# BEYOND AIRLINE DISRUPTIONS

*To Raston, Neo, Moena and Cassius, with hope that you will embrace uncertainty, remain curious, radiate love and never forget to dream.*

# Beyond Airline Disruptions

JASENKA RAPAJIC

ASHGATE

Published by
Ashgate Publishing Limited
Wey Court East
Union Road
Farnham
Surrey GU9 7PT
England

Ashgate Publishing Company
Suite 420
101 Cherry Street
Burlington, VT 05401-4405
USA

www.ashgatepublishing.com

**British Library Cataloguing in Publication Data**
Rapajic, Jasenka
  Beyond airline disruptions
  1. Airlines - Management 2. Crisis management
  I. Title
  387.7'42'068

ISBN: 978-0-7546-7440-5

**Library of Congress Cataloging-in-Publication Data**
Rapajic, Jasenka.
  Beyond airline disruptions / by Jasenka Rapajic.
    p. cm.
  Includes bibliographical references and index.
  ISBN 978-0-7546-7440-5 (hardcover) 1. Airlines--Management. 2. Aeronautics, Commercial--Management. I. Title.
  HE9780.R37 2008
  387.7068--dc22

2008030038

Mixed Sources
Product group from well-managed forests and other controlled sources
www.fsc.org Cert no. SA-COC-1565
© 1996 Forest Stewardship Council

Printed and bound in Great Britain by
MPG Books Ltd, Bodmin, Cornwall.

# Contents

*List of Figures*     *vii*
*List of Tables*     *ix*
*Preface*     *xi*

Introduction     3

Chapter 1     Obscured by Clouds     5

Chapter 2     Clearing the Way     21

Chapter 3     Hidden Causes of Operational Disruptions     47

Chapter 4     Organising Disruption Information     69

Chapter 5     Streamlining Disruptions     97

Chapter 6     Managing Disruption Losses     121

Conclusions     139

*Appendix 1: Standard IATA Delay Codes*     *143*
*Appendix 2: Resolving the 'Technical' Delay*     *147*
*Appendix 3: Crew Shortage*     *149*
*Appendix 4: Cost Saving and Cultural Issues*     *151*
*Appendix 5: Disruption Audit*     *153*
*Appendix 6: Direct and Indirect Cost of Aircraft Damage*     *157*

*Bibliography*     *159*
*Index*     *163*

# List of Figures

Figure 2.1    Disruption properties                                                    21
Figure 2.2    Operational events                                                       23
Figure 2.3    Aircraft departure measuring points                                      25

Figure 3.1    US airline's punctuality comparison, 2007 vs 1987–2007
              (on time arrivals)                                                       48
Figure 3.2    Punctuality trends at Heathrow airport (total scheduled
              operations and by selected airlines) 2002–2007                           67

Figure 4.1    Basic elements of disruption information system                          75
Figure 4.2    Disruption information system – basic concept                            83
Figure 4.3    Disruption information system scheme                                     90
Figure 4.4    Investment in accuracy                                                   92
Figure 4.5    Relational action map for disruption management                          94

Figure 5.1    Punctuality vs profitability, comparison of airlines with
              different operating models                                               99
Figure 5.2    Comparison of punctuality and length of delay for long-haul
              operators, traditional and low cost, on London–Newark
              route                                                                   101
Figure 5.3    Decision making process                                                 115

Figure 6.1    Disruption risk evaluation chart                                        131

# List of Tables

Table 1.1    Comparison of criteria used in various published delay
             reports                                                    12
Table 1.2    Extracts from US consumer reporting systems disclosing
             the airline data                                          14
Table 1.3    AEA Consumer Report (January–December 2007)               15
Table 1.4    Delay cost estimates                                      16

Table 2.1    Traditional direct and indirect cost structure            35
Table 2.2    Traditional structure of variable, fixed and indirect
             operating cost                                            35
Table 2.3    Punctuality cost structure                                39
Table 2.4    Delta cost structure                                      39
Table 2.5    Operational events and cost relationship                  42
Table 2.6    Example of errors in delay reporting                      45

Table 4.1    Operational event distribution                            76

Table 5.1    Disruption measures                                  112–114

Table 6.1    Identifying cost critical reasons for disruptions         134

# Preface

# Fasten Your Seat Belts for a Journey Beyond Airline Disruptions

I have been drawn to the subject of airline operational and cost inefficiencies for quite some time now. By being in a position to look at disruption problems from various perspectives, I found that knowledge about true root causes and costs of disruptions can become an indispensable tool for effective leadership, planning, and management, and help airlines to decrease the level of self-induced uncertainty. My passion for the subject inspired me to write this book in the hope that it will contribute to the easing of disruption problems.

While writing *Beyond Airline Disruptions*, I was certain that I wanted to name the changes in planned operations as 'disruptions', unlike many airlines and industry consultants who have introduced terms like 'punctuality issues', 'transportation events', or 'variance', to soften their negative aspects. The truth is that disruptions *are* damaging events that create losses, and cause inconvenience to airline customers, but also create learning opportunities. They must be fully recognised as such in order to attract the attention of managers at top organisational level – the only place from which disruption problems, that are cross-functional by nature, can be resolved.

So, welcome to the journey *Beyond Airline Disruptions*, a place where more light is being shed on the obscured area of airline management. This book does not offer a solution to specific disruption problems. It has been written to broaden the horizons for those involved or interested in airline business, and open up new opportunities for cost savings and improvements in on-time performance and loss recovery and improvements in on-time performance.

My interest in this subject followed my career path, spanning strategy, network, fleet and schedule planning, marketing and operations, within legacy, low cost and charter airlines. I have devoted many years to create methods that will help airlines identify tangible and intangible causes and costs of disruptions that spread wide across airline organisation. I was especially interested in their intangible aspects, including things like leadership, system knowledge, cross-functional communication, and cultural issues – factors that have the most profound impact on the extent of operational disruptiveness. The more deeply I got immersed into the obscured area of disruptions, the more obvious it became that the level of uncertainties and difficulties increase exponentially with complexity that is often created unknowingly during the planning processes.

I strongly believe that these self induced complexities and many other disruption issues can be better controlled with the support of methods for disruption loss management which will be introduced in this book. This knowledge needs to be underpinned with sufficiently accurate hard information that will help airline executives to focus on the most critical disruption events. In addition to quantitative methods for disruption management, the book will address some of the mapping techniques in support of intuitive reasoning, which is necessary to manage complexities associated with disruption loss management. These methods are among very few remaining competitive weapons that can significantly cut costs and recover losses, while improving airlines' operational efficiency.

Let us now fasten our seatbelts and begin the journey of discovery into the hidden dimensions of disruption loss management, from which, I sincerely hope, you will gain much inspiration for your further work in this area.

'If I had a formula for bypassing trouble, I would not pass it round. Trouble creates a capacity to handle it. I don't embrace trouble; that's as bad as treating it as an enemy. But I do say meet it as a friend, for you'll see a lot of it and had better be on speaking terms with it.'

Oliver Wendell Holmes

# Introduction

The quality of operational performance and extent of its deviations from original plans are invaluable indicators of airlines' financial health. What better way could there be to manage complex systems than to discover things that do not work well, and understand their causes and consequences. If recognised early enough, these deviations, that we will here call disruptions, can help prevent unpleasant surprises at a later stage. *Beyond Airline Disruptions* is written to establish the foundation for the new concept of disruption loss management, and explain how to turn knowledge about disruptions into a powerful business control tool. The focus is on identifying disruption losses and linking them with their root causes, which can help improve the quality of planning and decision making at all levels across an airline, be it strategic, financial, network planning, scheduling, or operations.

The opening chapter, 'Obscured by Clouds', describes the industry problem and explains what it is that holds airlines back from delivering more cost efficient, punctual, and regular services to their customers. The multi-dimensional character and uncertainty associated with the airline business make it difficult for airlines to adhere closely to their operational and financial plans. This situation is exacerbated by the absence of disruption information – a variance between planned operations and actual results. It leaves airlines and industry executives without sufficient knowledge about operational changes, their causes and costs, making it impossible to fully control disruption losses, improve flight punctuality and regularity, and minimise safety risks. As the only source of industry information about flight irregularities, delay reports do not fulfil their basic function. Chapter 1 reveals the weaknesses and narrow scope of the traditional reporting system, with real life examples. It brings to light report limitations, questionable quality of output, the lack of harmonisation across the industry and raises the question about their value and suitability for decision making and industry benchmarking.

Chapter 2, 'Clearing the Way', describes the disruption basics by describing the characteristics of main disruption properties, and explains how to identify, capture, and organise them so that they can form a solid base for the creation of a reliable disruption information system. It introduces the definition of cost driven disruption events, explains the direct causes of operational changes and goes more deeply into the structure of disruption costs. It further discusses how much of the disruption data we really need and how accurate it has to be to make up the optimal balance between their usefulness, volume, accuracy, and cost effectiveness.

In Chapter 3, 'Hidden Causes of Operational Disruptions', we will shed more light on the area of currently hidden causes of disruptions of a cross-functional nature, which will reveal a high level of interdependences between internal functions These causes have a 'relational' character and any effort to resolve them will create bonds between functional areas and strengthen the organisation.

Obtaining a full picture of the causes and consequences of flight disruptions requires the development of highly refined diagnostic methods of monitoring and questioning, to determine the detailed flow of disruptive patterns, and a sophisticated information system that will support such requirements. Chapter 4, 'Organising Disruption Information', describes the concept for disruption information management, the structure of a new disruption information system, its functionalities, and technology solution. It explains how to link costs with disruption events and their root causes, reveal, and prioritise the core problems. These links will break many of the departmental boundaries, make disruption information available to decision makers across the airline and raise cost awareness among the management and staff.

Chapter 5, 'Streamlining Disruptions', describes the ways airline operations can be made less disrupted and more cost efficient. It examines how much the simplification and focus on important issues can help airlines to streamline their operations, explains how to use a disruption information system to measure the efficiency of airline operations, and look at some management and organisational issues that are prerequisite for successful implementation of methods for disruption loss management.

An effective approach to disruption management and control assumes a well organised knowledge system that enables both the qualitative and the quantitative approaches to the problem solution. Once such a system is set in place, it starts to create new opportunities for airlines to act on what matters, and communicate important business issues across the organisation. By being able to get early warnings about the most disruptive elements of planned operations, managers can start to tackle disruption problems in a more efficient way on both a short- and long-term basis.

Chapter 6, 'Managing Disruption Losses', provides an insight into how best to use the acquired knowledge in practice. It explains how to identify disruption risks and problems beneath the surface, how to use disruption strategies to cut losses and improve flight punctuality and regularity. It also describes how to use the disruption information tool to recover losses caused during disruptions generated by third parties. Better understanding of the real causes of airline operational inefficiencies will help improve the quality of information and decision making across the industry.

# Chapter 1
# Obscured by Clouds

In this book, operational disruptions will be defined as deviations from originally planned operations expressed through variance in operational parameters, costs and revenue. Much of these deviations are reactions to external events, some are results of internal oversights, while some are caused by proactive actions taken to align business with ongoing changes.

Disruptions are rarely the result of random chance, except in cases of unavoidable acts of nature, or other catastrophic events that are not within the scope of this book. Their root cause is usually a consequence of human action, indicating that they can, to some extent, be controlled and that the organisation can learn from failure and modify them accordingly. Disruptions should be viewed as an opportunity to examine their origins, and costs, and to put in place measures to eliminate or reduce the risk of them recurring.

The concept of disruption loss management described in this book represents the basis for improvements in planning and decision making, especially in complex industries like air transport. It is emerging as an important part of business strategies, recognised in other industries as 'constraint management', 'failure detection and analysis' and 'operational risk management', among many others. The banking industry have even set the international standards for operational risk management, defined as the risk of losses resulting from inadequate or failed internal processes, people, and systems or from external events.

By introducing this concept into their management practices, airlines can improve control over dynamic changes of their operations and minimise associated losses. As it will be explained later in this book, disruption loss management requires a new mindset – a fundamental shift in the way operations are planned, managed, and controlled.

In the text that follows, we will describe current practices in airline disruption management and explain what prevents airlines from delivering more punctual and less costly operations.

## Operational Constraints and Their Implications on Airline Performance

Every day airlines depart late, cancel and divert flights, affecting millions of passengers worldwide. At the same time, they generate tens of billions of Euros annually in disruption losses, making traditionally thin profit margins even thinner. What holds airlines back from delivering more punctual, more regular, and less costly operations? To answer this question we need to dig deeper into the grey area of airline disruption management.

Airlines make tremendous efforts to plan their operations, compromising between numerous conflicting requirements. This is a complex and laborious work, where strategic goals are being incorporated into the network, schedule, and corporate plans, the main determinants of the quality of operations and its overall efficiency. By the time myriads of operational, tactical, and strategic constraints are harmonised, approved, and published in airline schedules, many external and internal inputs have changed. Each of these changes distorts the originally designed system, and continues to do so throughout the planned period. In the absence of tools and methods, airline executives are left deprived of the key information for disruption loss control, widening the gap between strategic and operational planning processes.

This raises many questions about the quality of airline management. How can business goals be planned down the line if, say, 20 per cent or more of total costs and their reasons is unspecified? How serious and insurmountable are the broken links between the operational–corporate–strategic functions within each airline and how can they be repaired? How comprehensive and accurate is the information airlines provide to air transport policy makers and how it does reflect back on them?

An airline that unknowingly spends almost half a million Euros to recover from one of many few days' long disruption events, has little chance to improve its operational procedures, organisation, communications, planning and management practices that have contributed to these losses, if management attention is focused on reported 'technical problems', only the last in the chain of delay reasons visible to the operations controller at the time of reporting.

In order to better understand the scope of disruption problems we need to take a closer look at their external and internal determinants.

*External constraints*

During the last decade, the airline industry went through a business transformation unprecedented in scale, stimulating a massive increase in air travel. The fast expansion strategies have started to seriously outstrip the pace of infrastructural development, especially in already congested areas. They have deepened the industry problems related to shortage of competent staff and management, affecting the quality of airline planning, management and control. Growing restrictions in the operational environment are leaving airlines with less space for errors and inefficiencies. At the same time, the depleted 'low-paid' knowledge is making them more prone to mistakes, thus fuelling the increase in the absolute number and length of flight disruptions and associated costs.

Airline tendencies to expand in the areas with already critical infrastructural and resource limitations are increasing their operating costs while decreasing the on-time performance. This has started to affect even the best 'low-cost' performers, pushing their on-time performance closer to low industry standards, with additional revenue needed to cover the higher costs.

Another business transformation that has had a profound effect on the structure and costs of operational disruption is the outsourcing of the non-core businesses. The quality of airline operations has become more dependent upon external vendors, over which airlines have lost direct control. Apart from traditionally independent service providers like ATC[1] and airports, the list of external suppliers is extending towards key operational activities – passenger handling, aircraft maintenance, IT and catering services shaping the quality and costs of airline output. Some of the most damaging disruption events in the past few years were linked with problems related to external service providers like ATC, airports and outsourced ground and IT services. They typically cause massive, days' long disruptions, affecting tens or even hundreds of thousands of passengers each time they occur.

*Internal obstacles*

By moving more closely to airline internal practices, we can see that despite technological advances, accumulated industry knowledge, and simplification of business models, airlines generally do not have an organised system to track disruptions, their causes, costs, and the effects they have on revenue. Unforeseen changes cause many executives to accept a great deal of waste in operating costs – they may be hiring more staff than they need to support the unnecessary changes, overpay for faulty subcontracted services, operate a route network that is not synchronised with available resources or overprice their products, without being aware of their full financial consequences.

*Self-induced and uncalculated disruption risks*  A great number of airline operational irregularities are created internally during the process of strategic planning. Whenever an airline decides to expand its services to highly congested airports, operate a diversified fleet, introduce multiple maintenance and crew bases, overutilise capacities, increase airline dependency on outsourced services or decide to lay off its workforce, and is not aware about its operational capabilities, it increases the level of uncalculated business risks. Each of these factors may become a potential source of further disruptions, and continue to affect operations throughout the scheduling period. On the surface, however, they may appear as 'unpredictable events' hidden behind operational causes like crew shortages, technical problems, ramp incidents, or any one of one hundred or more coded reasons.

This does not mean that airlines should not extend operations to busy airports, have more than one aircraft type in its fleet, or outsource many of its operational services. These strategies have a chance to succeed as long as top managers are

---

1   Air Traffic Control.

aware about the full consequences of disruptive services on airline costs and on-time performance, and price their product competitively. Knowledge about the most damaging root causes of disruptions can help airlines to re-examine the effectiveness of business strategies at all levels, such as network and fleet structure, resource utilisation, outsourcing policies, investment strategies, contractual obligations, loss recovery and many more.

Other self-induced risks include operational and planning oversights, errors and omissions, poor management practices, organisation, training, communication and airline culture, which are rarely assigned as causes of operational disruptions. These problems need to be observed and analysed as a part of a wider context described through principles of disruption loss management later in this book.

*Management, organisation and communication*   When operations do not go according to plan, we see airline managers seeking answers to the wrong questions. They gather reams of unreliable data on delays and their reasons expecting to find answers for poor operational performance, without realising that they may not be looking in the right direction. They cannot hear the right signals from noise made by 'delay reporters'. Delay meetings are a good example of how much valuable management time is wasted on analysis of insignificant delay events that could be resolved at the operational level. They often include simultaneously available but unrelated problems, solutions, goals, interests, and concerns. So, a meeting called to discuss disruptions may become discussion about staff absenteeism, a dysfunctional computer unit, route network inefficiencies, vendor's omissions, level of passenger compensation, individual responsibilities or outsourcing policies. The quality of the management decisions very much depends on how they allocate their time and what they choose to look at in the absence of methods for problem prioritisation.

The volatile operational environment requires continuous 'fine-tuning' between front-line and strategic levels, which does not function well. Front-line managers, often immersed in details, are generally more concerned with quick daily fixes through things like schedule recovery, or staff absenteeism. They are not in a position to fully understand the effects their decisions have on other parts of the organisation and, most importantly, on airline costs. They are quite satisfied with the information contained in delay reports, which pretty much depends on their own input. Senior managers, however, tend to be more concerned about financial performance measures like costs and profits – information that is not contained in operational reports. They work and think at higher levels with often 'vertically distorted' vision: looking down is much like watching the earth from the airplane – it looks spacious, peaceful and orderly, right up to the moment they land.

Strategic and operational managers often communicate with difficulties, as they do not speak the same language. The activities of these two groups, supported by the measures they use, create a chasm of misunderstanding. In the absence of links between strategy and operation, airline executives remain short of information about the root causes of operational problems that may require their attention or are, unknowingly, caused by them through the process of strategic or commercial planning. This is especially important when reasons for disruptions are conceived in the back offices or by strategic planners. They are normally among the most costly ones, as they systematically disrupt the daily schedules. At the operational level, all efforts are directed at improving operational performance within the boundaries of the existing system. But, who is it that decides how to best align the characteristics of the operational environment with business and organisational goals? How good are these decisions?

There are situations where senior managers try to bridge this gap by intervening randomly in critical situations without the substantial knowledge necessary to resolve such complex situations. The consequences are often damaging for an airline, as shown in the following example. It was not before the US low cost carrier JetBlue experienced embarrassing service disruptions, cancelling nearly 1,200 flights and reporting a $30 million loss over five days that the top executives realised the destructive effects of the airline's operational weaknesses and absence of strategic inputs, and which contributed to a change in airline leadership.

On the other side, there is a strong resistance from operations managers to any kind of external interference and control of their decisions, made under constant pressure. They insist that airline operation is inherently random and unique. Managers who have been used to enjoying the protection that lack of information and performance measurement provides, may be reluctant to view their operations through a more powerful lenses.

All these problems are pretty much induced by the lack of system information about disruptions, their costs and their root causes. Let us dig more deeply into the current status of disruption information systems.

*Knowledge and information*   Existing operations control systems are designed to provide generic information about flight delays and cancellations, good enough to fulfil the airline public requirements, but far from sufficient to manage the business.

The creation of a disruption information system requires currently non-existing links of operational, scheduling, cost and revenue information with their root causes. Existing software solutions are designed around non-integrated business processes, by developers who work for different organisations. In order to sustain as businesses, vendors are inclined to design generic solutions, rather than to satisfy more costly needs of individual airlines. The attempts of a variety of external consultants to fill up this information gap have failed to produce satisfactory results for reasons explained later in this book.

Other, more complex solutions, such as optimisation tools designed around operational and cost issues, are still in their infancy. They are costly to implement, and their results impossible to measure and compare. Some of them have caused major disruptions and massive, months' long, flight cancellations. Many vendors' attempts to measure disruption costs by associating them with operational changes have failed, including the EU-funded, three years' long project, and will continue to do so until airlines introduce a bottom-up approach to cost management and integrate these costs with operational parameters of planned and actual information.

In the absence of well structured and comprehensive disruption information, airlines use very basic delay information to measure the quality of operational performance. The following real life example illustrates the power disruption information could have on airline decision making:

An airline was complacent with their operational achievements published in the annual report. Maintenance reliability scored high, crew shortage problems were 'pronounced' tolerable and other causes of delays were considered minor. This did not sound right to a sceptical senior executive aware of the high increase in operating costs but unaware about their reasons. He decided to re-examine the quality of reporting on operational performance with the help of an experienced analyst. It was soon discovered that over 70 per cent of delayed flights were operated as a reaction to unknown primary reasons, hiding the real causes of disruptions. The major disruption events were reconstructed, recreating their links with primary causes, by use of the disruption information tool. Based on these findings, it appeared that the airline was suffering from serious problems associated with aircraft maintenance and crew shortages, the main causes of days' long irregularities, including flight cancellations, diversions, positioning flights and hired replacement aircraft. They managed to identify not only the root causes of disruptions, but also their costs. The analysis revealed a high level of hidden costs related to crew shortage, which were the source of number of costly reactionary disruptions. Over half a million Euros was spent just in one week to recover from flight disruptions, and to compensate passengers on heavily delayed and cancelled flights. It was further discovered that the real causes for many of the operational problems were hidden behind poor planning, problems with internal communication including serious disputes, lack of operational procedures and insufficient staff training.

Let us now see how the lack of information about disruptions affects industry reporting and benchmarking.

*Industry reporting*

We normally tend to look at operational problems through their causes and effects while in reality, cause and effects are often blurred due to distorted inputs. What we can see is only a part of what happens by looking at inferior, uncorrelated delay reports. The elementary delay information is compiled and published by three major providers of air services – airlines, airports and ATC. Each of them uses their own definition of basic operational parameters and various disruption properties to measure their own effectiveness, making it difficult to define system inefficiencies, and impossible to use them for industry benchmarking. This slightly resembles the situation that Sir Josiah Stamp described, as follows: 'Public agencies are very keen on amassing statistics – they collect them to the nth power, take the cube root and prepare wonderful diagrams. But what you must never forget is that every one of those figures comes in the first instance from the village watchman, who just puts down what he pleases.'

However strange it may sound, no official aggregate statistics about flight delays exist at a European level. The attempt by the European Commission (CAPRS Project), intended to provide information on punctuality and other service quality indicators to industry and the general public, ended unsuccessfully in 2005. The main reason for failure, as stated in the final report, was airline unwillingness to provide the required information. Only 16 out of 51 invited airlines took part in the Project. Even these 16 airlines did not supply all the required data. Among the reasons for airlines' rejections could be a conflict of political and business interests, as well as narrow scope and a simplistic approach to a complex industry problem.

Public reports on flight delays sourced from airports and airlines are published by various government agencies, airline organisations, and ATC services, or compiled by on-line regional data providers. They are segmented in a variety of ways and are difficult to compare for previously explained reasons. The diversity of criteria applied in periodical delay reports published by AEA[2] (30 airline members of which 25 report on punctuality), ERA[3] (63 airline members of which 31 report on punctuality), IACA[4] (38 charter airlines), Eurocontrol, government agencies in some countries (CAA[5] in the UK, DGAC[6] in France), regional Internet information providers such as www.flightontime.info in the UK, and www.flightstats.com in the USA is shown in Table 1.1.

None of these reports is comparable – they overlap and have a different scope and content. This situation only mirrors the internal state of punctuality information within airlines. The lack of standardisation allows individual interpretations and adjustments.

The importance of accurate reporting on causes of disruptions is best described by US experts, who have said that failure to pinpoint the causes of delays and cancellations aggravates the situation and contributes to a steady decline in the airline industry's credibility with the public. In 2000, the US Federal Aviation Administration (FAA) set up a Task Force to define criteria for airline reporting on disruptions and their causes, hoping that enhanced data collection will help airline and industry planners to do their jobs better. Since 2003, this information is reported each month to the Department of Transportation's Bureau of Transportation Statistics (BTS) by the 20 US air carriers that have at least 1 per

---

2    Association of European Airlines.
3    European Regions Airline Association.
4    International Air Charter Association.
5    Civil Aviation Authority.
6    Direction Générale de l'Aviation Civile.

**Table 1.1    Comparison of criteria used in various published delay reports**

| Delay parameters | AEA | ERA | IACA | Eurocontrol | CAA UK | flightontime.info |
|---|---|---|---|---|---|---|
| On-time performance measure | Delay ≤ 15min | Delay ≤ 15min | Delay ≤ 15min | Delay > 5min ≤ 15min | Delay ≤ 15min | Delay ≤ 15min |
| Flight regularity | Yes | Yes | No | No | No | No |
| Delay length categorisation | Departures/Arrivals delayed more than 15min | Within 60 min | Departures delayed more than 15min | Flights delayed more than 15min and more than 60 min | 16–30min / 31–60min / 61–180min / 181–360min / 360+min | Within 15min / 1h+ / 3h+ |
| Average delay | Yes | No | Per movement and per delayed flight | Yes | Yes | Yes |
| Aggregate delays per individual airline | Yes | Yes | No | No | Yes | Yes |
| Reasons | Delays>15min; Pre-flight preparation; Maintenance/equipment failure, airport and ATC, weather, reactionary | Within 60 min; Ops, weather, ATC; Passengers, aircraft/technical, reactionary, other | Delay reasons: 19 reasons; Primary departure delay reasons; Airline, airport; En-route; Weather; Security, misc | Primary departure and arrival delay reasons; Airline, airport; En-route; Weather; Security, misc | No | No |
| Airport delays (departure and arrival) | No | No | No | Yes | No | Yes |
| Delays per city pair (min per movement) | No | No | No | Yes | No | Yes |
| Delays per individual airline and airport | Yes | No | No | No | No | Yes |
| Flexible reporting | No | No | No | No | No | Yes, plus customised reports on request |

cent of total domestic scheduled-service passenger revenues. The reports cover non-stop scheduled-service flights between points within the United States.

Unlike the US, the general public in Europe is deprived of the information about the nature and sources of airline delays and cancellations, described by many airlines as 'commercially sensitive'. In reality, this information is not available – not only to the general public, regulators, industry analysts and policy makers – but often to the airlines themselves. The comparison of the criteria used in European (AEA) and US (DoT[7]) public reports is shown in Tables 1.2 and 1.3.

Airline managers and staff waste long hours discussing the causes and responsibilities for poor operational performance, because the scope of knowledge and information required to resolve the complex operational issues relies on narrow departmental views with lack of clearly defined responsibilities. In addition, delay reports often contain errors and omissions, the majority of which are created during manual data input (delay reasons, departure and arrival times), and include a great deal of subjectivity. Very often, however, wrong input is caused by lack of instructions, absence of standards and procedures, weak links between planning and operations management and control. By bluntly accepting the information contained in delay reports we are taking part in the illusion that we understand the causes and consequences of operational failures.

*Implications on costs*

The damaging effects of system constraints, manifested through airline operational disruptions, have direct implications on airline costs and quality of service. Among the biggest obstacles to resolving critical disruption issues is the lack of information about cost consequences caused by the reliance on traditional financial reports, which fails to shed light on underlying business problems. In many ways, the lack of information about disruption costs is the result of an outdated industrial approach to cost planning, applied to one of the most dynamic and most complex industries. Airline accountants may need to know the cost of passenger compensations, for instance, but an executive looking to reduce these costs would also need to know which flights were disrupted in the first place, and why. Variance in volume of hired capacities is also important: did the number of subchartered aircraft rise because of increased demand, for example, or because of problems with available crew resources, or maybe with technical reliability? Financial metrics fail to detect these important distinctions. Airlines must have the opportunity to dig more deeply through their conventionally structured financial costs in order to discover and monitor the root causes, bringing more understanding than would be possible with current financial reporting.

As a result of lack of reliable information about disruption costs sourced directly from airlines, there is a myriad of confusing, potentially damaging reports

---

7   Department of Transportation.

## Table 1.2 Extracts from US consumer reporting systems disclosing the airline data

### CAUSES OF DELAY

| Carrier | Total Records | Air Carrier Delay | % Air Carrier Delay | Extreme Weather Delay | % Extreme Weather Delay | National Aviation System Delay | % National Aviation System Delay | Security Delay | % Security Delay | Late Arriving Aircraft Delay | % Late Arriving Aircraft Delay |
|---|---|---|---|---|---|---|---|---|---|---|---|
| 9E | 22290 | 1028 | 4.61% | 73 | 0.33% | 1484 | 6.66% | 3 | 0.01% | 861 | 3.86% |
| AA | 53472 | 2988 | 5.59% | 435 | 0.81% | 5072 | 9.49% | 12 | 0.02% | 3659 | 6.84% |
| AQ | 3763 | 145 | 3.85% | 1 | 0.03% | 7 | 0.19% | 0 | 0.00% | 129 | 3.43% |

### LIST OF REGULARLY SCHEDULED FLIGHTS I/ ARRIVING LATE 80% OF THE TIME OR MORE PER AIRLINE

| Carrier | Flight Number | Orgin-destin. Airports | Scheduled Departure Time | Number of Operations Reported | Percentage of Flight Operations Arriving 15 Minutes Late or More D/ | Number of Min Late Average | Median |
|---|---|---|---|---|---|---|---|
| F9 | 513 | LGA-DEN | 2140 | 29 | 82.76 | 64 | 55 |
| OO | 5961 | ORD-PIA | 1645 | 29 | 82.76 | 59 | 50 |
| MQ | 4231 | HSV-ORD | 1925 | 29 | 82.76 | 55 | 41 |

### FLIGHT CANCELLATIONS PER AIRLINE

| Carrier | At 32 Reportable Airports | | | |
|---|---|---|---|---|
| | Number of Airports Reported | Flight Operations Scheduled | Flight Operations Cancelled | Percent of Operations Cancelled |
| AMERICAN EAGLE | 18 | 24,254 | 1,994 | 8.2 |
| PINNACLE | 16 | 8,406 | 713 | 8.5 |
| MESA | 23 | 12,212 | 812 | 6.6 |

*Source*: US DoT, Air Travel Consumer Report

## Table 1.3    AEA Consumer Report (January–December 2007)

PUNCTUALITY

| AEA Carriers | Total Short/Medium Haul | | | | | | | Long Haul | | | | | | |
|---|---|---|---|---|---|---|---|---|---|---|---|---|---|---|
| | N° of flights performed | % on-time arrivals | | % on-time departures | | Flight regularity | | N° of flights performed | % on-time arrivals | | % on-time departures | | Flight regularity | |
| | unit | % | rank | % | rank | % | rank | unit | % | rank | % | rank | % | rank |
| AF - Air France | 501 477 | 82.1 | 7 | 81.5 | 8 | 98.1 | 20 | 55 528 | 63.7 | 13 | 61.6 | 14 | 99.2 | 10 |
| AP - Air One | 90 804 | 65.8 | 24 | 73.7 | 22 | 99.0 | 11 | | | | | | | |
| AY - Finnair | 79 292 | 81.0 | 10 | 80.6 | 11 | 99.4 | 6 | 5 941 | 70.5 | 9 | 68.7 | 13 | 99.2 | 10 |
| AZ - Alitalia | 252 802 | 74.7 | 17 | 77.9 | 17 | 97.9 | 23 | 13 298 | 71.6 | 8 | 74.5 | 6 | 99.2 | 10 |
| BA - British Airways plc | 235 182 | 64.7 | 25 | 67.5 | 26 | 98.0 | 21 | 60 126 | 56.2 | 18 | 61.5 | 15 | 99.4 | 7 |
| BD - bmi | 121 085 | 79.4 | 12 | 81.5 | 8 | 98.8 | 15 | 1 732 | 73.8 | 7 | 76.2 | 4 | 99.0 | 13 |
| CY - Cyprus Airways | 15 606 | 64.3 | 26 | 70.6 | 24 | 99.6 | 5 | | | | | | | |
| EI - Aer Lingus | | | | | | | | | | | | | | |
| FI - Icelandair | 6 896 | 66.3 | 23 | 76.8 | 19 | 100.0 | 1 | 2 595 | 69.2 | 10 | 76.7 | 3 | 100.0 | 1 |
| IB - Iberia | 357 520 | 77.8 | 15 | 81.3 | 10 | 98.8 | 15 | 17 718 | 64.1 | 12 | 70.2 | 11 | 99.6 | 5 |
| JK - Spanair | 99 866 | 62.9 | 27 | 71.3 | 23 | - | | 656 | 36.6 | 20 | 44.2 | 19 | - | |
| JP - Adria Airways | 21 154 | 73.9 | 18 | 73.8 | 21 | 99.7 | 4 | | | | | | | |
| JU - JAT Airways | 19 975 | 75.6 | 16 | 79.6 | 15 | 97.9 | 23 | | | | | | | |
| KL - KLM Royal Dutch Airlines | 182 333 | 84.9 | 2 | 80.5 | 12 | 98.5 | 18 | 31 052 | 76.4 | 2 | 71.7 | 9 | 99.4 | 7 |
| KM - Air Malta | 16 668 | 68.6 | 22 | 67.5 | 26 | 99.8 | 2 | | | | | | | |
| LG - Luxair | 11 655 | 86.6 | 1 | 88.1 | 3 | 98.0 | 21 | | | | | | | |
| LH - Deutsche Lufthansa AG | 619 131 | 81.2 | 9 | 80.2 | 13 | 98.9 | 13 | 49 067 | 74.3 | 4 | 73.0 | 8 | 100.0 | 1 |
| LO - LOT Polish Airlines | 86 481 | 73.9 | 18 | 76.4 | 20 | 98.3 | 19 | 2 989 | 56.3 | 17 | 54.5 | 17 | 99.8 | 4 |
| LX - Swiss International Airlines | 116 874 | 79.3 | 13 | 78.2 | 16 | 98.9 | 13 | 13 428 | 75.6 | 3 | 73.5 | 7 | 99.3 | 9 |
| MA - Malev Hungarian Airlines | 49 606 | 84.0 | 4 | 83.1 | 7 | 99.1 | 8 | 1 085 | 64.4 | 11 | 71.5 | 10 | 98.3 | 16 |
| OA - Olympic Airlines | 86 447 | 68.9 | 21 | 68.9 | 25 | 98.7 | 17 | 1 779 | 62.8 | 14 | 59.6 | 16 | 99.9 | 3 |
| OK - CSA Czech Airlines | 72 982 | 81.8 | 8 | 88.6 | 2 | 99.1 | 8 | 1 392 | 73.9 | 6 | 86.4 | 1 | 99.0 | 13 |
| OS - Austrian | 155 248 | 84.1 | 3 | 83.7 | 5 | 99.1 | 8 | 6 761 | 82.1 | 1 | 79.5 | 2 | 99.5 | 6 |
| OU - Croatia Airlines | 22 244 | 72.8 | 20 | 77.5 | 18 | 97.6 | 25 | | | | | | | |
| RO - Tarom Romanian Airlines | 13 568 | 82.2 | 6 | 88.8 | 1 | 99.8 | 2 | | | | | | | |
| SK - SAS Scandinavian Airlines | 291 757 | 80.6 | 11 | 80.1 | 14 | 97.6 | 25 | 6 338 | 74.3 | 4 | 76.0 | 5 | 99.0 | 13 |
| SN - Brussels Airlines | 70 906 | 83.1 | 5 | 83.4 | 6 | 99.0 | 11 | 3 434 | 58.3 | 16 | 51.7 | 18 | 98.0 | 18 |
| TK - Turkish Airlines | 151 714 | 79.1 | 14 | 83.8 | 4 | - | | 9 470 | 59.5 | 15 | 69.2 | 12 | - | |
| TP - TAP Portugal | 75 153 | 59.5 | 28 | 62.5 | 28 | 99.4 | 6 | 11 200 | 40.3 | 19 | 42.5 | 20 | 98.1 | 17 |
| VS - Virgin Atlantic Airways | | | | | | | | | | | | | | |
| AEA | 3 824 426 | 77.7 | | 78.9 | | 98.5 | | 295 589 | 65.9 | | 66.7 | | 99.4 | |

and studies circulating around the industry. Some of these cost estimates are shown in Table 1.4.

### *Implications on passengers*

Passenger disruptions are more complex to monitor than flight or aircraft disruptions, and can significantly outweigh them. They are very much dependent on network connectivity, cancellation rates and booking policies and cannot be measured by existing flight delay statistics. Passengers on cancelled flights could be transferred to another airline, experience long delays, or just left to resolve the problem themselves. Lost customer loyalty caused by poor flight punctuality and regularity is a hidden cause of direct and, even more, indirect longer-term consequences on revenue that can ruin an airline's reputation and even cause its demise.

It has been estimated that about 78 million passengers, carried by over 30 AEA member airlines in 2007, have experienced flight delays longer than 15

**Table 1.4    Delay cost estimates**

| Disruption cost type | Source | Cost estimate |
|---|---|---|
| ATC delay costs, US – 12 years projections | FAA | $170 billion |
| Disruption costs, annual, US | FAA | $22 billion |
| Cost per minute of delay | Eurocontrol/ITA | €39.4–€48.6 for airlines |
| Cost per minute of delay | Eurocontrol/ Westminster University | €72 based on ATFM delays, network average – delays over 15min |
| Costs per minute of delay | Roland Berger | $70 |
| Cost of en-route ATFM delay per minute | Eurocontrol | €40–€60 ATFM delays |
| | | €28 reactionary delays |
| | | €46–60 passenger costs |
| Delay costs, annual | Economist survey – Europe | $10 billion |
| Delay costs – US domestic 2007 | Joint Economic Committee, US Senate, 2008 | € 41 billion, cost to airlines, passengers and the US economy |
| Delays costs US, largest airlines, domestic operations, annual | ATA | $3.7 billion |
| Delay cost, annual | Booz Allen and Hamilton | €100–400 million for a top-ten European airline |
| Costs per minute of delay | Major European Airline | € 600 wide-body |
| | | €150 for 120 seater jet |
| Direct and indirect delay costs | Booz Allen and Hamilton | 0.6%–2.9% of revenue, depending on the size of operation and method of calculation |
| Delays and cancellations | Boeing | $5,000 for single-aisle aircraft $11,000 for double-aisle aircraft |
| Delay cost per seat | Airbus | $75 for 3 hr delay to $110 max over 6 hours (wide body); Between $32 and $60 per seat for over 3 hrs (single-aisle A320) |
| Direct costs of aircraft damage, annual | Flight Safety Foundation | $5 billion with related disruption costs being 'several times higher' |
| Disruption costs caused by bird strikes, US, annual | Bird Strike Committee USA/Canada | $1.2 billion |

minutes, while about 3.7 million passengers were forced to make alternative travel arrangements due to flight cancellations. The magnitude of the problem gets completely lost in delay reports, where for example, 1 per cent in annual decrease of flight punctuality for European airlines passes almost unnoticed, while in reality it affects over 3 million passengers. Passenger inconvenience cannot be easily measured, but it can obviously be quite damaging for the industry. It can also shape the future development of air transport industry in many areas.

The attempt of the European Union to protect passengers by using regulatory measures, did not improve the situation. The introduction of punitive and ambiguous legislation, strongly opposed by airlines, has left an ever-increasing number of disrupted passengers struggling harder to get compensation for inconvenience caused by flight cancellations. On the other hand, introduction of the Regulation has revealed many system weaknesses, and has opened vigorous debate about responsibilities for inefficiencies of the air transport system, which may contribute to future improvements.

*Implications on safety*

Airlines operating through congested airports and airspace are faced with increased safety risks. The number of ground and airborne incidents is constantly increasing. Things are getting worse under continuous pressure to deliver on time, but also because of limited infrastructure, the decreasing number of skilled workers and well known problems with outsourced services. This leads to costly consequences, especially those related to aircraft and equipment damage, and injuries to personnel.

One of the key elements for incident prevention is an in-depth understanding of disruption causes. When it comes to safety, the widely spread practice of waiting for an incident to happen and then resolve the problem is simply not tolerable. Disruption risk assessments need therefore to become an integral part of the process of quality control.

The following examples from CHIRP, the UK Confidential Human Factors Incident Reporting Programme (www.chirp.co.uk), which publishes safety-related information reported anonymously by flight crew, air traffic control officers, licensed aircraft maintenance engineers and cabin crew, illustrate how the constant pressure on airlines to operate on time can increase safety risks:

> Report from captain about commercial pressure: On one occasion, I was despatching a wide-bodied aircraft belonging to a contracted third-party operator. The Station Manager for the airline, as usual, was applying pressure for an on time departure. On this particular occasion I did not re-check the fuel load figures until after the aircraft had departed, only to find that up-lift was short by 5,000 lb. I now insist on re-checking my figures before signing-off the fuel log. I understand that the airline has a salary bonus scheme, in which the Station Manager's performance is based largely on Station punctuality record.

Report from air traffic controller: At AAA (hidden airport code) there is a night jet ban, which comes into effect at 23:29 hrs local … I regularly have aircraft call up at 23:15 hrs and say they are doing their best to get to the departure runway on time. There are a number of factors, which act against them in these scenarios:

- The aircraft are parked at stands, which often involve a long taxi to the holding point.
- They are large jets, which have longer load times.
- The aircraft often route in similar directions putting pressure on ATC to get them away.

In the past, we [ATC] have been made to instruct aircraft, occasionally at the holding point, that they are not allowed to depart and have to night stop. This is primarily not an ATC restriction but an airport one. It often leads to heated exchanges on R/T (communication between pilots and air traffic controllers over radio) which is far from ideal. I fully sympathise with the crews who feel hard done by when they are not allowed to depart and likewise for the passengers. On occasions, I have seen aircraft taxi at very high speed to get airborne before this jet ban. Will they have carried out their pre-flight checks in a similarly rushed manner? The night jet ban at AAA is something, which puts undue pressure on both airlines and ATC and could be better handled by Airport Authority.

*Implications on the environment*

Disruptions at congested airports and airspace have been marked as considerable generators of noise and also air pollution caused by increased en route, take-off, approach and taxi times and consequently higher fuel consumption. According to IATA[8] and ELFAA[9], inefficiency in air traffic management accounts for approximately 12 per cent of airline greenhouse gas emission. This complex global problem will take time to resolve. Among many undertaking scientific, economic and political action, airlines need to continuously search for the most critical causes of flight disruptions. By minimizing the number and length of operational irregularities, they will make necessary contributions to a reduction in the amount of gaseous emissions.

---

8   International Air Transport Organisation.
9   European Low Fares Airline Association.

## Who Pays For and Who Benefits From Operational Disruptions?

As we have already learned, operational inefficiencies are in many ways caused by unresolved industry issues. Despite this, the costs generated by disruptions are borne almost solely by airlines and passengers. It is sometimes suggested that commercial service providers like airports and ATC, whose profits are linked to the number of handled aircraft movements, would be inclined to ignore punctuality and even acceptable safety standards in the interests of increased profit. In addition to airports and ATC, the list of service providers for which airline disruptions make good earning potential in the short term, include hotels, aircraft handlers, airport shops, ground transport providers, aircraft lessor and insurance companies any or each of which can benefit every time long flight delays or cancellations strike airlines and passengers.

To resolve this issue, we need to create a system that will differentiate financial responsibilities for disruptions among airlines and service suppliers. Once airlines are in control of the root causes and losses caused by flight disruptions, they will be able to more equally share this cost burden with external suppliers and, more importantly, to set the priorities for system improvements.

## Where Should We Look For Improvements?

The concept of airline disruption management offers a new opportunity for cost saving, better quality of services and airline performance in general. To achieve this, it is necessary to dig beneath the surface, right down to the source of the problems, with the support of smartly designed systems and knowledge networks spread throughout the organisation. The responsibility for operational performance should be brought closer to corporate level, which is best able to determine what trade-offs between quality and costs are acceptable for managing expectations of future results.

While sophisticated optimisation tools necessary to help solve the information problem are still a remote option, airlines should adopt a more realistic approach towards a solution that will provide essential, less complex but more effective operation. This will help them build the much needed cost awareness and 'system' thinking among decision makers, resulting in less risky and more profitable operations.

The chapters that follow will explain the basic elements of operational disruptions and introduce new methods for disruption management, aimed at the improvement of operational strategies, decision-making and ongoing operational and cost efficiencies.

# Chapter 2
# Clearing the Way

In very essence, operational disruptions are the results of strategies that fail to match operational capabilities and leave little or no space for soothing the effects of internal inefficiencies and unpredictable events. How seriously can they affect airline financial results? This important business question cannot be answered by looking at traditional management reports. As we have seen so far, the narrow approach to disruptions seen mostly as delays and cancellations proved ineffective in mitigating their negative impact on airlines and other parties involved in the process. Airlines that focus on delays as the only aspect of disrupted operations are missing important element of business information – the full effects of operational changes on airline operating costs and revenue.

There are lots of ambiguities related to disruption management. Disruption properties are not clearly defined, nor organised into a system that will make them recognised as a measure of airline operational efficiency. In this chapter, we will describe the elements that constitute disruption information and 'clear the way' for creation of system for disruption loss management.

## Disruption Basics

The first step in creating a more comprehensive disruption information system is to identify its basic elements, necessary for better understanding of changes in planned operations. These elements are essential for the creation of a disruption information system that will integrate operational and cost data, and establish missing links between strategy and operations.

There are three basic determinants of disruptions: operational events, disruption costs, and disruption causes, as shown in Figure 2.1.

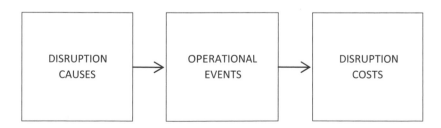

**Figure 2.1    Disruption properties**

Once these core disruption properties are linked and organised into a single system, they will create a foundation for disruption management, allowing airlines to identify changes in planned operations (operational events) and their cost consequences, leading to a better understanding of the root causes of these changes. This will create opportunities for a new, more dynamic approach to planning, management, and control of airline operations. In the text that follows, we will explain event properties, go more deeply into the structure of disruption costs, and describe underlying causes of disrupted operations.

*Operational events*

Operational events are the result of unexpected factors manifested through changes in flight schedules, including those related to altered aircraft and airports (even when flights operate on time). They are the backbone of a disruption information system and show how an airline responds to changed circumstances. Each of the operational events can incur changes in costs and revenue, directly or indirectly. However, the information about events alone does not tell us much about what caused them in the first place, and how efficiently the airline resolved the disruption problem. They are just a part of the system that can provide comprehensive information about disruption effects on an airline's operational and financial results.

There are six basic types of operational events crucial for capturing the information about changes in planned cost, revenue, flight punctuality, and regularity: flight delays, flight cancellations, flight diversions, aircraft changes, aircraft rentals, and additional flights (Figure 2.2). Their time-span and frequency could vary significantly – from short delays measured in minutes or hours, to less frequent but more costly disruptions, which could be days, or even months long. Capturing the relevant data about events, their causes and consequences, and organising them into a single information system is the prerequisite for effective disruption management.

*Flight delays*  Flight delays occur when an aircraft departs or arrives late compared with the published schedule. They are an important indicator of the quality of airline services. Nevertheless, airlines do not know much about their true root causes and consequences. Airline managers spend too much time searching for solutions to these problems by looking at unreliable delay reports. They are short of information that can help answer the basic questions about reasons and costs of deviations from the original plan, and as such do not have much business value.. Improvements in delay reporting, including their integration with costs and root causes could bring huge benefits to airlines. However, delay information can only become a powerful indicator of airline operational efficiency and the service quality if it forms an integral part of a disruption information system. If properly organised and integrated, it could help airline managers to recognise internal and external weaknesses, and bring a new dimension to operational and strategic decision making. In order to achieve this goal, airline executives must

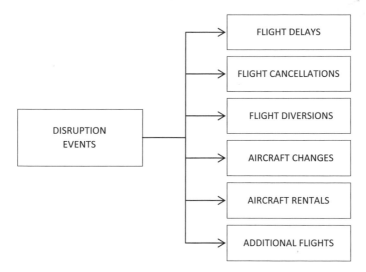

**Figure 2.2    Operational events**

become aware of the problems associated with delay reporting at both airline and industry level.

Let us now take a look at how airlines, airports, and ATC define and measure delays, and what kind of information we can find in various industry reports. We will be focusing on multiple references to schedule parameters, look at the effects of schedule buffers on delay reporting, examine the consequences of unreported delays, learn more about problems related to data capturing, and take a closer look at delay issues from passengers' perspective. Once we understand the obstacles to better reporting on delays, we will be able to tackle the specific problems more successfully and create a healthy ground for the integration of delay information into a system for disruption management.

*Schedule references*
Despite seemingly simple definitions of flight delays, there are many ambiguities in the reporting on late departures and arrivals by individual airlines, airports, and ATC. Each of these reports is based on different references which suite their individual needs and is not comparable. Additionally, organisations that compile the industry figures and produce public punctuality reports usually apply their own rules for data collection. In absence of clearer industry guidance, numerous arbitrary assumptions used to define delay parameters, result in questionable quality of published reports, and less credible industry benchmarking. In order to cope with the influx of delay reports from a diverse number of sources, it is very important to understand their origins, and specific rules applied for each of those reports. Let us now look at these issues in more detail.

Departure times could be captured at various phases of the departure process: when the aircraft door is closed at the gate, power switched on, chocks removed, brakes released, aircraft pushed from the gate, or when it starts to move under its own power. Arrivals are usually measured from the point when the aircraft makes a final stop at a gate or parking stand after landing, after engines have been switched off, or when it stops at the gate or the remote stand. However small these differences may seem, they can affect the statistical reporting on punctuality. For example, if an airline measures departure from taxi-out rather than brake release, an average time lapse of, say, 5 minutes between the two can 'improve' on-time performance records every time actual departure remains inside the 15 minutes interval, the point from which airlines officially report a flight as delayed.

From an airline perspective, published schedule changes represent the difference between the latest published schedule and actual departure or arrival times. For this purpose, some airlines compare the actual data with schedules that include changes up to 24 hours before flight departure, while others use the extended period of up to 3 days (72 hours) before the planned day of operations. For various planning purposes, airlines may use either budget or seasonal schedules as reference points for measuring deviations from planned operations.

From passengers' perspective, scheduled times of departure and arrival are those published at the time they originally booked the flight. Any further changes close to the departure time may be considered as flight delays and may need to be used by airline customer services to resolve passenger complaints and compensation claims.

References used by airports and ATC add to their diversity. Airports rely on publicly available information about planned schedules, like those published in global distribution systems (GDS), which may not always be up-to-date. Actual departures and arrivals are usually calculated as a sum of airborne times and estimated taxi times. ATC may use the latest take-off slot in an airline's flight plan and actual airborne time as a base for delay calculation. As a result, the same flight could be recorded as 'on-time' and 'delayed', depending on the statistical source. The diversity of delay references is illustrated in Figure 2.3.

Obviously, the number and duration of reported delays will vary depending on the choice of reference schedule and a purpose of delay reporting. In this book, we will be focusing predominantly on improvement in reporting on airline delays as a part of disruption loss management.

*Schedule buffers*
As a response to the growing number of flight delays at congested airports, airlines are building the most predictable delays into their schedules. In this way, they are trying to avoid late arrivals, especially critical for passengers with tight connecting times. If a flight routinely experiences a 20-minute wait in a departure queue and those 20 minutes are added into its flight schedule, it will continue to be delayed for 20 minutes, but will show as 'on time' in a punctuality report and may never be further scrutinised as delayed. Calculating delays with reference to

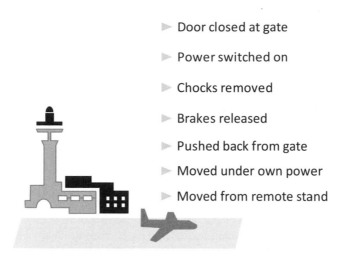

Door closed at gate

Power switched on

Chocks removed

Brakes released

Pushed back from gate

Moved under own power

Moved from remote stand

**Figure 2.3    Aircraft departure measuring points**

padded planned schedules significantly underestimates the delay problem. How many delayed flights are 'hiding' behind the schedule buffers? According to the report published by the US Joint Economic Committee (JEA), when padding is removed from the analysis, total delays are actually 57 per cent higher than the US airlines operating domestic services report. Similar situation is in Europe where, according to Eurocontrol, 45.4 per cent of flights departed later than 5 minutes, while 21.9 per cent were delayed by more than 15 minutes of their scheduled departure. At the same time, 42.4 per cent of flights arrived later than or equal to 5 minutes, with 21.4 per cent being delayed by more than 15 minutes (Eurocontrol, Annual Report 2006). Apart from losing on productivity, this practice is making it more difficult for airlines to identify true causes and consequences of delays and heavily distorts the airline benchmark figures. This also means that punctuality comparisons between network and point-to-pint carriers need to be noted with caution. The on time performance of network carriers is actually worse than is shown in published reports, and works in favour of low cost carriers with simplified operating models.

*Unreported delays*
While airlines can internally measure punctuality from a zero-delay reference for their internal needs, in public reports flights are counted as delayed if they are 15 or more minutes late compared to the reference schedule. This widely accepted 15 minutes 'grace' period for delay reporting (14 minutes in the US) means that a flight is still counted as departing on-time if the plane leaves the gate within 15 minutes. Used across the industry, this 'delay free zone' has become one of the operational and commercial constraints, because:

- The 15 minutes 'grace' period ignores the distinction between operational and commercial values of short and long-haul flights, where value of, say, a one-hour short-haul flight that is delayed for 25 per cent of the actual block time (majority of European domestic routes), cannot be compared with a long-haul flight where the 15 minutes period may take just 2.5 per cent of the whole journey.
- For most passengers it is departure punctuality that defines their impression of an airline's on-time performance, even if it is all too obvious that on-time arrivals are important for connections and the execution of the schedule plans. Telling them that they have departed on-time, while departure was 15 minutes delayed, on a 45 minutes long flight, does not seem appropriate.
- It sets an example that inefficiencies are tolerable. It is hard to expect that other performance targets within the airline should be set close to 100 per cent when the whole industry holds that 15 minutes delay is tolerable, or when wiping off 25 per cent of flights delayed between 0 to 14 minutes has been accepted as an industry standard.
- This 'grace' period does not allow for true reporting on causes of delays. For example, a flight delayed for 14 minutes will not be registered as late even if it caused a longer delay due to the missed ATC slot.
- It creates additional tension between airlines, airports, handling companies and ATC during the already highly intensive and insufficiently synchronized aircraft departure process, where each of the involved parties tend to satisfy their company's or their individual interests, affecting the accuracy of delay reporting, especially on delay causes.

*Problems with data capturing*

The quality of delay reports are dependant, to a great extent, on manual data input, which is prone to subjectivity due to diverse personal, departmental and company interests. Airline policies in defining the references for capturing delay information are not always quite clear to those responsible for data input, resulting in inaccurate reporting on flight delays.

It seems that the clarity of some input parameters for delay reporting has not improved much for decades. Pilots' internet forums are awash with questions about the way pilots should report on flight departure and arrival times should be recorded – an area that airlines and regulators have so far failed to clarify. Similar questions were raised back in 1989 during an extraordinary case, when a pilot was accused of misusing the definition of 'flight time'. He was reporting on a departure, when after taxiing, the aircraft returned for a technical check due to a false alarm, and then resumed the schedule using the same clearance. In the hearing before the US National Transportation Safety Board, the pilot and the administrator could not agree about what these definitions really referred to, revealing ambiguities in the standard definition of departure and arrival times. The pilot's appeal was granted but only after a thorough investigation.

Emerging technologies are, however, finally laying foundations for improvements in delay reporting. The automated aircraft equipment like ACARS (Aircraft Communications Addressing and Reporting System) has a potential to significantly improve accuracy of recorded departure and arrival times. In the US, number of airlines using the system is on the constant increase. Based on the information available to DoT in September 2008, 65 per cent of the 20 reporting air carriers use ACARS exclusively, while majority of remaining airlines use the combination of ACARS and manual reporting systems. Using the ACARS, still does not guarantee completely unbiased input – pre-set reference points from which actual departure and arrival times are measured remain dependent on airline policies. Furthermore, airlines that impose harsher consequences for delays on their staff may be subjected to a more inaccurate data inputs, even with the automated system in place, like some pilots' practices of releasing the aircraft brakes early in order to prevent delays from being electronically recorded. The problem is about to be minimised or completely eliminated with the new generation of ACARS where wheels will be able to 'sense' a ground speed of more than 3 knots, to avoid the system to be 'fooled'. This, however, cannot prevent practices of some airlines operating from busy airports to leave the gate within the 15 minutes 'grace period', move aircraft to the remote stand waiting for the late take-off slot, and report that the flight has departed on time. It must be mentioned that, in some cases, airlines are forced to leave the gate before they get the departure clearance and park at stand, in order to release the space at congested gates.

There are atypical delay events that are not included in the existing delay information systems. They are usually not systematically recorded or are not recorded at all, like in case of flight cancellations, diversions and tarmac delays – events that more concern passengers than airlines. It has been discovered only recently that DoT reports, for example, did not include tarmac delays, as in the case of JetBlue events at JFK on Valentine's Day 2007, where 130,000 people were held 'hostages' in the planes due to bad weather for up to 10 hours, and then cancelled. Or, when in December 2007, 101 of American Airlines and American Eagle planes from California were diverted to Austin and other points, and then sat on the tarmac for at least 5 hours. These types of disruptions were statistically recorded as 'diverted' or 'cancelled', or sometimes not recorded at all, regardless of the fact that passengers had sat on planes for hours. Despite claims that the number of tarmac delays is small, these flights still carry millions of passengers with unpleasant experiences. Following several extreme 'tarmac' incidents, and huge public pressure, the Air Transport Association (ATA), the trade association of leading US airlines have introduced a rule, amending the BTS (Bureau of Transportation Statistics) reporting data with original gate departure time of the aircraft and the total ground time away from the gate, in the event that aircraft subsequently return to the gate. The U.S. Department of Transportation will also collect additional data elements when flights are cancelled and diverted, or experience gate returns. These rules have been implemented to offer consumers a more accurate portrayal of arrival and tarmac delays.

*References used for public reporting*

Airlines are generally cautious with public disclosure of delay information due to its commercial value. Periodical delay reports are partly accessible through their professional associations or government agencies, which individually may apply different criteria for data collection. Each of the airlines, airports and ATC look at delays from a different perspective and use different references to report on delays. Let us now see what delay references are used and how they are defined by some of the industry organisations and information providers. This information gathered from public sources may look inconsistent – but it only reflects the confusing situation with delay reporting in the air transport industry.

The Association of European Airlines (AEA), the biggest airline association in Europe, defines actual departure and arrival times as 'points when the aircraft leaves from, or arrives at its parking stand – flights within 15 minutes of schedule are not regarded as delayed, but as on-time... Any change in schedule up to 3 days before the planned day of operation is taken into consideration.' The AEA Consumer Report is based upon a voluntary commitment by the members of the Association to report on delays using the commonly defined standards, different from those applied by individual airlines, which prompted AEA to worn its members that 'any similar statistics reported by airlines, which are not part of the AEA Consumer Report should not, under any circumstances, be construed as representing a fair comparison with the figures presented herein. AEA cannot guarantee the accuracy of such figures and indeed has reason to believe that they may represent entirely different performance criteria.'

The European Regions Airline Association (ERAA) publishes comprehensive airline delay reports, based on voluntary submissions. It defines on-time departures as flights departing within 15 minutes of their scheduled departure time, while the choice of reference schedule parameters depends on individual airline practices.

The Civil Aviation Authority (CAA) UK compiles figures in cooperation with airports and Airport Coordination Ltd (ACL). Actual times of operation are derived from the air transport movement returns made by airports to the CAA. The planned times supplied by Airport Coordination Ltd include changes made up to 24 hours before operation. When the two sets of data are matched, if an airline appears to operate a series of flights significantly 'off slot', the Aviation Data Unit will substitute information from published timetables (where such are available) in place of the ACL slot data. Because the planned time of operation relates to the arrival/departure time at the stand, whilst the actual time of operation relates to wheels on/off the runway, the taxi time is estimated according to information provided by ACL or the airport. For example, estimated taxi times for Heathrow airport are: 10 minutes for arrivals and 20 minutes for departures; for Gatwick: 10 minutes for arrivals and 15 minutes for departures; for Stansted: 5 minutes for arrivals and 10 minutes for departures.

Eurocontrol defines delay as the duration between the last take-off time requested by the aircraft operator and the take-off slot given by the central flow management unit, with an addition for estimated taxi time. Flights are counted as delayed when they are delayed for more than 5 minutes. Eurocontrol's CODA (Central Office for Delay Analysis) incorporates operational data received from various operators, compiling and publishing the information contained in delay reports supplied voluntarily by a number of airlines.

The U.S. Department of Transportation's (DoT) Bureau of Transportation Statistics (BTS) provides information about airline on-time performance, flight delays, and cancellations. It is based on monthly data filed by airlines each month with the Department of Transportation's Bureau of Transportation Statistics (BTS). According to BTS, a flight is counted as 'on time' if it operated less than 15 minutes after the scheduled time shown in the carriers' Computerized Reservations Systems (CRS).

The BTS's reportable delays recorded in OPSNET (Operations Network), or air traffic delays, are defined as 'delays to Instrument Flight Rules (IFR) traffic of 15 minutes or more experienced by individual flights, which result from the ATC system detaining an aircraft at the gate, short of the runway, on the runway, on a taxiway, and/or in a holding configuration anywhere en route.' Such delays include delays due to weather conditions at airports and en route, FAA and non-FAA equipment malfunctions, the volume of traffic at an airport, reduction to runway capacity, and other factors. Flight delays of less than 15 minutes are not reported in OPSNET.

Internet information providers like flightaware.com and flightstats.com, publish the live and summary overviews about delayed flights. They collect information from 'a large number of sources (governments, airlines, airports, and others)'. Delay references are based on actual airborne times and estimated ground times with reference to various published schedules. Delay information depends on the flight-tracker's messages (contains information for flights controlled by air traffic control). Whenever the tracker's message is not received, the information is estimated. Due to the nature of data gathering, delay data published by these information providers often does not match the airline records.

There are industry organisations that are not involved in the publication of delay information, but their definitions of actual schedule time references shape the quality of delay reporting. Here are two examples:

The International Air Transport Organisation (ICAO[1]) defines actual departure and arrival times through definition of *block-to-block* times, as 'the moment the aircraft is pushed back from the gate or starts taxiing from its parking stand for take-off to the moment it comes to a final stop at a gate or parking stand after landing'.

The European Aviation Safety Agency (EASA) in its Crew Flight Time Limitations papers describes departure and arrival times through the definition of actual *flight time*: 'when the aeroplane first moves under its own power (excluding push-back) with intention of taking off until it next comes to rest on its parking

---

1    International Civil Aviation Organisation.

spot after landing', the definition that majority of industry sources define as 'block time'.

Once we learn the ways public delay information is generated, we will be able to better understand the differences in reporting from various sources, and learn how to read them. For instance, one should be aware that the number of flight delays shown in ATC reports may be lower than the number of airline delays because of difference in reporting references explained earlier in this chapter. In addition, the volume of delayed flights is associated with their primary causes will always be lower than those recorded by ATC – if, say, the first of four planned daily flights is delayed due to ATC, both the airline and ATC will associate this flight with an ATC cause. At the end of the day, an airline will assign the four flights to the ATC reason, while ATC will make the same assignment of ATC reason for delay just for the first flight.

Distorted information about disrupted operations makes it difficult for industry professional to understand their true extent. Sometimes, high number of operational disruptions is being justified by the increase in volume of flights, hiding the true scale of the industry's problem. The following statement made during the testimony of the US Federal Managers Association (FMA 2000) sheds more light on the magnitude of operational problems:

> We are faced with complex problems in the areas of scheduling, equipment, data acquisition, airspace design, and technologies both old and leading edge. An overall 8 percent increase in operations from 1995 to 1999 should in no way increase the number of operational errors by 53 percent, operational deviations by 47 percent, runway incursions by 73 percent, or delays by 58 percent during the same period. The relationship is quite obviously far from linear.

*Delays from passenger perspective*
During the last decade, the quality of passenger services has significantly deteriorated in all phases of the journey, adding to the already high costs of passenger travel measured in money and time. The following major shifts in passenger travel experience have emerged as the most damaging ones:

- Extension in unwanted waiting times spent in airborne holding stacks, during check-in and security checks, in planes waiting in taxiing queues and at remote stands.
- Decline in quality of passenger information about flight delays and cancellations, post-flight information about their reasons, and often lack of credible and systematic comparative information across air carriers, which will allow passengers to make on-time performance comparisons in support of their travel choices.

The number of passengers experiencing long waits at remote stands before departure, as well as after arrival, is growing rapidly at the world's top airports.

The US Federal Aviation Administration (FAA) reports that taxi-out times longer than one hour, at JFK airport, doubled in 2007 compared with the previous year, leaving about 5,000 passengers 'stranded' in long ground queues every day. Airborne delays are also on the increase, adding to passenger anxiety. According to British Airways[2], total passenger delay minutes from airborne holding alone (at Heathrow airport in 2004) amounted to 2,295 passenger delay hours per day – or 287 passengers holding for 8 hours every day, assuming there are approximately 100 passengers per flight.

Airline sensitivity to public exposure of their poor delay records is understandable – there were situations in the past when just one heavily publicised incident has had a final impact on changes at an organisation's top or even the demise of an airline. However, leaving the public and industry professionals without basic information about airline-specific delays and their causes could be at least equally damaging – like in Europe, where comparable aggregate reports and delay information per individual airline are not publicly available. The protectiveness of airline delay information seems to get over the top when One of the major airline associations introduced special rules to protect confidentiality of airline delay information, explaining that 'in the wrong hands it [delay information] can be misinterpreted to the disadvantage of the airline'! In the US, however, information about delays is much more transparent and is regularly reported by major domestic carriers and 32 biggest airports.

Problems with delay reporting are obvious, as is the need for their improvement at industry level. From airline side, by getting a more realistic and thorough picture about delayed operations, airlines will be better positioned to improve overall performance and improve travelling experience of their passengers.

*Flight cancellations*   Flight cancellations do not happen very often. Statistically, the volume of flights cancelled on the day of operation rarely exceeds 2 percent of the total number of delayed flights shown in regularity reports. While this number represents a small percentage of total flights, it has an impact on a large number of passengers counted in millions. In 2007, cancellations of 'just' 1.4 per cent of scheduled flights caused inconvenience to about 5 million passengers carried by 26 reporting AEA airlines. The total number, however, would be much higher if 'pre-planned' cancellations were taken into account. Whatever the reason, flight cancellations have a serious impact on passenger loyalty in the short and in the longer term periods.

Airlines cancel flights for a variety of reasons, mostly due to technical and operational problems, or bad weather conditions. Cancellations can also be a consequence of strategic and management oversights such as overoptimistic planning that did not take into account airline operational limitations, or failed implementation of new software solutions. The decision to cancel a flight requires

---

2   British Airways response to a CAA consultation on the report of the Aerodrome Congestion Working Group, April 2005.

careful consideration of alternative solutions, as it may cause huge passenger dissatisfaction and attract media attention. Sometimes, under pressure to resolve problems quickly, airlines may decide to cancel a series of flights in order to prevent longer knock on effects. Decisions about flight cancellation require fine balancing between a variety of operational, commercial and cost parameters – information which is currently not readily available at operational level.

Airline reports typically do not contain sufficient and well organised information about flight cancellations, additional costs and associated loss of revenue, especially when cancellations occur at outstations. This may create problems with loss recovery and with passenger compensation claims and, more importantly, make managers short of experiential knowledge that may influence their future decision making.

*Flight diversions*   While the number of diverted flights may be insignificant in comparison with other operational events, these flights can be costly for airlines and generate a great deal of inconvenience to passengers. A flight is considered diverted when aircraft is forced to change its intended destination for a variety of reasons including bad weather, airport capacity constraints, sudden airport closures or landing restrictions, medical emergencies, aircraft malfunction, the need for refuelling and many more. Diverted flights are followed by 'diversion recovery flights', defined as return flights from the diverted airport to the original destination, or any other airport chosen by the airline. They may require introduction of substitute aircraft to accommodate diverted passengers, cause longer crew and aircraft delays and displacements, disrupt other planned flights, generate additional costs associated with passenger and crew accommodation and transport, passenger compensation claims, and result in loss of passenger goodwill. Reporting on diverted flights is usually not consistent due to atypical input, and depends very much on ability of software application to handle this data, and on input procedures. ASTA, the world's largest association of professional travel agencies, said it is 'particularly important to include the data on diverted flights (in US DoT reports)... this data may be hard to collect, as the Air Transport Association claims, but every effort should be made to get it so the manner in which these events occur, and their impact on the public, can be better understood.'

*Aircraft changes*   Aircraft changes are made to minimise negative effects of disrupted operations caused by unserviceable aircraft, or to better adjust to market fluctuations using the internal aircraft and crew resources. Consequences of aircraft changes depend on factors such as fleet structure and age, tightness of schedule plan, availability of spare aircraft and crew, additional number of maintenance and ground handling staff, aircraft performance, seat configuration and so on. Airlines that hold spare aircraft, spare crew, or operate loose rotations to minimise disruption risks have already built additional cost of aircraft change into their fixed costs, even though these spare capacities may not always help them to efficiently resolve the disruption problems. The most common changes in variable costs occur when swapped aircraft is of a different type and size than the missing aircraft: if the replacement capacity is smaller, it may cause the loss of revenue from denied passengers, while bigger aircraft can incur additional costs. The volume of these costs could be high if accumulated over time. As an example, an aircraft swap on a medium haul route once a day could cost an airline more than €1.5 million over a year in fuel only (based on increased fuel consumption of 1t tonne per block hour). This could become a large loss generator if not justified by additional revenue.

*Aircraft hire* Resolving disruption problems by hiring external capacities is a costly solution. Sometimes, however, it is the only option left to operational decision makers to avoid long delays and flight cancellations. Aircraft could be hired to replace units that become unserviceable due to technical faults, because of damage, crew shortage or to bring spare parts from another technical base. Aircraft can also be hired if the originally planned capacities are delivered late from repairs, regular maintenance checks, by lessor or by manufacturer. Late deliveries of the new Airbus A380 and Boeing 787 were among the longest 'waits' in airline history, forcing many airlines to find alternative solutions, which for some of them meant strategic reshaping of fleet and even their marketing plans.

*Additional flights* Airlines may introduce additional flights from variety of reasons: to take stranded passengers back to the destination airport, ferry a temporarily repaired aircraft back to its maintenance base, operate flight without passengers on board because of technical problems, or to carry spare parts necessary to repair the aircraft experiencing problems at an outstation, if airline finds it financially justified. Introduction of these flights could cause further operational disruptions. They always generate additional costs, but this information is rarely systematically collected and associated with originally disrupted flights. The reasons for introduction of additional flights are often classified as unavoidable (weather conditions, operational conditions or technical faults), but in many cases, like in the following example, they can be caused by internal errors.

An indication of a technical problem shortly after the takeoff forced the pilot to fly the aircraft back to the departure airport. It appeared that the indication was false and airline was allowed to continue this ad hoc charter flight from remote destination only after complying with safety requirements from a Minimum Equipment List (MEL). After careful consideration of alternative solutions, the airline decided to operate the flight as soon as the MEL demands are fulfilled. This meant that containers with passengers' baggage had to be offloaded from the aircraft. As a part of the solution, an additional ferry flight was soon sent to bring the baggage back to the passengers. However, upon arrival the crew realised that the containers with passengers' baggage could not be uploaded before another set of containers, loaded in error at the base airport, were taken out from the aircraft, and left at this distant airport. The containers were later 'successfully' collected by another ferry flight.

*Disruption costs*

In today's world where cost competitiveness shapes the level of success or failure more than ever before, airlines are in need of new tools to guide them to unexplored areas of cost saving. One of the few remaining options is the control of losses caused by internal inefficiencies, manifested through operational disruptions.

Disruption costs are already built into the airline plans, but are hidden behind crew, maintenance, fuel, aircraft, handling and passenger costs, among others, making airline executives unaware about their real values. Some recent estimates have shed more light on this issue showing that disrupted operations drives a great proportion of airline costs. The Report *Your Flight Has Been Delayed Again* of the Joint Economic Committee (JEC[3]) of the US Congress revealed that in 2007 airlines operating domestic flights spent \$19 billion in fuel, labour and maintenance costs while aircraft sat idle or circled in holding patterns above congested airports. It has been estimated that the top-ten European carriers with on-time performance at around 75 percent carry between €100 and €400 million in annual delay costs (Niehues *et al.*, 2001). The ATH Group (Baiada, 2005) points out that the 'negative effect of the *variance* inherent with hub-and-spoke operation impacts the network airline's bottom line annually by upwards of 10 percent to 20 percent of total costs or more'. These figures could be much higher if all of disruption costs were included. Beyond these costs lays enormous potential for savings and improvement of airlines' operational efficiency.

*Current cost management*   The ability to quantify disruption costs and identify their causes can bring profound changes in airline planning and decision making practices. In order to get to that stage we need to understand current obstacles to disruption cost control, and examine more closely the traditional approach to operating cost management, which could briefly be described as insufficient to manage the business, unable to link costs with their root causes and in need of a new system approach.

The traditional approach to airline costs management is very useful for accounting and general management purposes. At the highest level, costs are allocated in a simple way following airline functional areas, and then grouped as direct and indirect, or fixed and variable. These cost breakdowns allow easy monitoring of an airline's overall performance, aircraft evaluation, or cost efficiency at departmental level, and are used for industry benchmarking. The cost structures are simplified to avoid complexities associated with allocation of cross-functional costs down to aircraft, route, sector, or type of services. Traditional airline costs, shown in Tables 2.1 and 2.2, are shaped by industry, internal needs, and government standards. This categorisation however, cannot answer one of the fundamental management questions – what drives the change in costs?

---

3   *Your Flight Has Been Delayed Again*, Report by the Joint Economic Committee, May 2008.

**Table 2.1    Traditional direct and indirect cost structure**

| DIRECT OPERATING COSTS | INDIRECT OPERATING COSTS |
|---|---|
| Flight operations | Station and ground expenses |
|     Flight crew salaries and expenses | Passenger services |
|     Fuel and oil | Ticketing, sales and promotion |
|     Airport and en route fees | General and administrative |
|     Insurance and aircraft rentals | |
| Maintenance and overhaul | |
| Depreciation and amortisation | |

*Source*: ICAO

**Table 2.2    Traditional structure of variable, fixed and indirect operating cost**

| VARIABLE DIRECT OPERATING COSTS | | INDIRECT OPERATING COSTS |
|---|---|---|
| Fuel costs | Fuel and oil – operational responsibility | Station and ground expenses |
| Variable crew costs | Crew subsistence and bonuses | Passenger services |
| Direct engineering costs | Related to flying cycles and flying hours | Ticketing, sales and promotion |
| Airport charges | Landing fees, airport charges | General and administrative |
| ATC charges | En route navigation charges | |
| Passenger service costs | Handling fees meals/hotel expenses | |
| **FIXED DIRECT OPERATING COSTS** | | |
| Aircraft charges | Depreciation, rental, insurance | |
| Annual crew costs | Salaries, flight and cabin crew administration, other expenses | |
| Engineering overheads | Engineering staff costs, maintenance administration, other overheads | |

*Source*: ICAO

*Note*: In comparison with the above ICAO structure which is used worldwide, US carriers use DoT Form 41 cost breakdown which provides a more detailed cost breakdown – cost data are broken down by fleet, maintenance costs are subdivided, and it is updated more frequently.

If we use apportioned costs per block hour, AKM, route, or per any other common denominator to make cross-functional decisions, like improvements in network and aircraft efficiency or investment in additional resources and equipment, we increase the risk of making the wrong decisions. Costs shown in traditional information systems are just a historic 'snapshot' of what was supposed to be the correct value at the time the budget draft was made. As soon as the 'budget schedule' starts to change, the relationships between direct and indirect, fixed and variable costs are also changed, making the calculated unit costs obsolete, and in some cases inadequate for decision making.

This may, at least partly, answer the question why airlines with long established practices make so many changes of planned operations once the season starts. We have seen traditional and even some low cost carriers incurring significant losses by reducing their operation by 2 per cent or more in the middle of season, due to 'overexpansion', 'overstretched capacities' or 'to avoid more operational problems'. What were the causes of such serious misjudgements resulted in change of strategic decisions made few months ago? How many of these changes and related losses could be associated with wrong evaluation of disruption risks, and poor understanding of system limitations?

The vague state of disruption information resulted in many, often simplistic attempts to quantify delay costs. Some of these estimates that are years and even decades old are still in use, and the emerging ones are the result of localised, random, and incomparable assumptions, which only add to the confusion, as shown in Table 1.4, Chapter 1.

The question is, if this is all so vague, how can airlines adequately plan their operating costs, and how can they use this information to adjust to the ongoing changes? Let us now look at a traditional approach to a costs planning process described by one former airline manager of a major network carrier:

> The typical process of cost planning starts with projected traffic, cost and revenue for the coming year. The company's finance director then sets a target figure for net results including the necessary return to shareholders. This is further broken down into management units and transmitted to senior directors, responsible for squeezing the savings out of their respective departments. The initial figure may be adjusted several times during the year. There are reviews after the IATA slot coordination meetings and regular refinements in the light of information received on forward bookings, interim revenues, and yields. These adjustments can result in even tighter cost controls. The intense cycle of setting targets and searching for further departmental cuts is giving an early warning if a director is going to exceed the budget. If this happens, there are generally negotiations between the director and the CFO's office to reach a satisfactory result. The process could be tightened further if necessary using various management techniques.

There are the two major setbacks in this process. The first one relates to sources of information used for cost projections for the coming year, based on too many assumptions. The second is the management aspect of cost control. Led by the nature of traditional cost information, managers put too much emphasis on cost control of departmental performance rather than on interrelated problem areas. As unforeseen problems start to emerge, senior directors have no other choice but to put even more pressure on middle managers and, through them on junior staff to save more. The next round of 'unexpected' events includes the reset of targets, and continual search for new cuts from already well 'squeezed' departmental cost.

What could be learned from the cost variance structured around functional areas shown in Tables 2.1 and 2.2? There are of course many well known principles for effective 'high level' cost planning and cost saving measures focused around single functions like, for example, fuel saving measures. Actions for fuel costs saving are normally assigned to the operations function. There is a whole set of principles airlines use to minimise fuel consumption. They include flying at optimum speeds and flight levels, tankering fuel at least expensive airports, careful weight and balance control or flying the 'cost efficient' air routes (not necessarily the shortest ones). In reality, however, most of these principles do not work. Fuel consumption will be increased every time when flight cannot operate at optimum flight level, ATC diverts the aircraft to a longer route, or put it on hold over the busy airport. Many of the reasons for increase in these costs may not be of operational nature. They could be the result of strategies that force expansion at congested airports and routes, where operations will be increasingly disrupted, and will keep aircraft consuming more fuel despite maximal efforts of crew and operations staff to apply the company's fuel saving policies. For them, this could be rather discouraging and may affect their future behaviour with regards to the cost saving measures.

In order to overcome these problems, airlines need to take a new approach to cost measurement that will more closely reflect the dynamics and functional dependencies of airline operations, and help them make cost efficient business decisions. In addition to looking at totals of operating costs, they should, for this purpose, focus on costs of change, and associate them with their underlying causes. This can be achieved by identifying operational events, their links with costs captured as close to the source as possible and further with their origins defined by direct and indirect causes of operational disruptions. This more dynamic approach to cost control will open the new opportunities for cost saving, focused around the most critical cross-functional problems.

*Defining the disruption costs*   The airline schedule, which is the base for the annual budget plan, is the result of the company's collective effort to provide the best service possible to their customers and make the most of available resources. Every change and adjustment in the planned schedule may shift actual costs away from planned targets. The size of the gap between expectations expressed through airline plans and dynamics of real operations depends on an airline's ability to evaluate disruption risks and, when circumstances change, be able to knowingly manage these changes. This ability can be measured through the variance between costs of planned and actual operations. Understanding this variance is the key for improvements in cost control, airline operational capabilities, and quality of services.

As we have seen earlier, the top-down approach to cost control is inadequate for cost calculation of operational changes. To get closer to this information the cost data must be associated with disruption events, and linked with their true root causes. Once costs of schedule changes are separated from other airline costs, new opportunities will be created for more dynamic planning and cost control.

*Disruption cost structure*    Disruption costs could be classified in the following two categories: punctuality and delta costs.

*Punctuality costs* are strategic investments in disruption prevention and are the part of airline fixed operating costs. They may include costs like spare aircraft, spare parts and equipment, additional crew, more operations staff, specific management information systems, investment in knowledge workers, and other costs aimed at minimising the risk of operational disruptions and achieving the longer-term improvements in punctuality and regularity. Punctuality cost breakdown is shown in Table 2.3. Much of these costs are caused by system constraints that will be described in this and the following chapter. They are planned at strategic level, and require a good understanding of variable part of disruption costs, defined as delta costs.

*Delta costs* are the variance between planned and actual costs related to schedule changes. They are caused by many factors and activities across the airline organisation and beyond. Some of this costs are included in airline contingency plans, while the majority, that create an integral part of variable operating costs, are not identified as such in traditional reporting systems. They are not recognised as a category of airline costs. The main obstacle for this recognition is an absence of system that will link delta costs with operational events and their root causes. This includes known operational risks, like predictable events that cannot be resolved in the short run like crew shortages, operations to congested airports, multiple crew and technical bases and other strategic issues. They could also be the result of unpredictable factors like unexpected delays in aircraft delivery, aircraft damages caused by third parties, or other external causes. Internally, they could be caused by unrecognised system weaknesses, errors, and omissions that are difficult to plan

Delta costs could be used to discover, minimise, or eliminate reasons for airline inefficiencies. As such, they represent an indispensable instrument for disruption management and control, and are an important element of a measuring system for airline operational efficiency. The structure of delta costs, or costs of change, is shown in Table 2.4.

Each of these costs is triggered by operational events and will be explained here in more detail.

*Route costs*   One of the main drivers of change in route costs is the change in block hours, caused by diversions from the planned route or change of aircraft type. Changes can also occur when aircraft is placed in 'holding pattern' queuing for landing, or when the optimal air route is redirected to a longer or more costly one. On some occasions, airlines chose to make longer trips to avoid high charges imposed by some countries, even if the flight is consequently delayed. Among other reasons that can affect the route cost, is the increase in fuel costs as a result of higher aircraft speeds intended to compensate for departure delays.

Each of these costs may not look significant until they start to accumulate. According to Eurocontrol, airlines spend 7.7 million minutes in holding stacks. Cost of fuel is estimated at €100 millions, five times higher than €20million allocated to ground delays. At airline level, British Airways' airborne holding at Heathrow airport (Seasons 2004/5) amounted to 298,904 minutes – the equivalent

**Table 2.3    Punctuality cost structure**

| |
| --- |
| Spare aircraft costs |
| Operations staff (crew, engineering, ground operations, flight operations, operations control) |
| Equipment and infrastructural costs |
| Investments in information systems |
| Investment in knowledge |

**Table 2.4    Delta cost structure**

| | |
| --- | --- |
| Route costs | ATC, fuel |
| Crew costs | Non-scheduled allowances, hotels, meals, transport, transfer |
| Airport charges | Landing, parking, security, other |
| Handling charges | Aircraft handling, passenger handling |
| Passenger costs | Passenger care, transfer, denied boarding compensation, delay compensation |
| Aircraft repair | Direct costs: temporary and final repair, spares, engine, third party, other |
| Subchartered aircraft | Aircraft hired as 'fully inclusive', 'ACMI', 'dry lease' |
| Revenue loss | Revenue lost to other carriers, denied passengers, refunds, sales on board |

of having approximately three aircraft unavailable for the whole season. The airline spent approximately \$2 million per month in fuel for air holding at Heathrow alone.

*Crew costs*    Changes in flight and cabin crew cost are accrued when their planned duty time is interrupted or has reached its limits due to flight delays, cancellations and diversions, and because of changes of aircraft type, introduction of additional flights or hired capacities. The magnitude of these costs is determined by disruption location, distance from the base airports, size of the aircraft, contracted accommodation and transport, additional crew numbers, and frequency of their occurrences, among others. They are expressed as costs of accommodation, meals, transfer, transport, non-schedule allowances, and crew rentals. On the less obvious side, crew costs will increase every time an airline expands its operation at hub airports, increase the number of crew bases, introduce more aircraft types, or experience crew shortages. Consequences of these strategies could be harsh for an airline and generate high losses, like in the case of a medium size European airline, which experienced six months of disrupted operations due to crew shortage, incurring €2.2 million in disruption losses.

*Landing and handling charges*    Airport fees that should be used for disruption cost calculation are driven by the type of aircraft, time of the day, number of passengers, additional parking hours, number of landings/take-offs and charges at diverted airports. They vary from airport to airport and depend on airport strategies and pricing policies for aircraft and passenger services.

*Passenger costs*    Passenger costs related to delays, cancellations and diversion include costs of passenger accommodation, meals, transfer, transport, recatering, and also refunds, denied boarding compensations and compensation for flight cancellations. Airlines operating from European airports may face additional compensation costs due to EU regulation on passenger protection, which entitles passengers booked on a cancelled flight to €250 to €600 compensation, depending on the length of their journey. It also obliges airlines to organise special care of passengers experiencing long delays and penalise them for each denied passenger.

*Cost of aircraft damage*    These costs relate to repair of damaged aircraft and can include temporary, final and third party repair, spares and engine, ferry and test flights, transport of spare parts, and other tangible and intangible costs like special lessor requirements, administrative expenses, decreased market value of aircraft and fuel penalties for changed aerodynamics. Events caused by aircraft damage often incur long and costly reactionary disruptions. The length of repair depends on the type of damage, airport location and inclusion of third parties. Some of repair costs could be offset by insurance compensations. However, the level of deductible values is quite high and is mostly borne by airlines.

*Cost of hired aircraft* The cost of subchartered aircraft depends on the availability of the required aircraft capacity at the time when it is needed to replace an unserviceable aircraft. Often, however, the available replacement aircraft does not match the original capacity and may have operational and technical limitations and therefore incur additional costs. Extra costs will also be incurred whenever the replacement aircraft is based outside the required airport. The cost of subchartered aircraft depends on the type of agreement between the two parties, and could be contracted as:

- Fully inclusive – includes all of the flying costs.
- ACMI – includes costs of aircraft, crew, maintenance and insurance, where airline pays for variable costs like fuel, ATC and airport charges.
- Dry lease – includes cost of aircraft, while airline bears remaining operating costs in full.

*Revenue loss and loss of passenger goodwill* Loss of revenue caused by operational disruptions includes losses incurred by disrupted passengers transferred to other carriers, denied passengers, refunds, lost baggage, and sales on board. Potential loss in revenue which is result of inconvenience caused to disrupted passengers, could significantly affect airline's longer term results. Some carriers consider this information as too 'soft' to be taken into serious consideration, while others are of the opinion that being able to evaluate the losses caused by disrupted operations can raise the awareness of management and staff about the decline in market share due to poor operational performace. Loss of passenger loyalty caused by flight disruptions depends on many tangible and intangible factors like type and location of disruption event, length of delay, travel alternatives, competition, frequency of flying, purpose and length of journey, the way disrupted passengers were handled by the airline and other service providers, and many more. These factors will surely have a significant impact on passengers' future decisions on whether to fly again with that airline or not.

*Disruption cost allocation* Each of the disruption costs is generated by one or more disruption events described earlier in this chapter. Linking the delta costs with disruption events is crucial for their quantification and also association with their root causes. Association between events and costs is shown in Table 2.5.

This association of costs with disruption events is crucial for bridging the gap between disruption costs and their root causes. The way this data can be collected and organised will be explained in Chapter 4.

*Disruption causes*

Running an airline only by knowing the financial results without any means of understanding their causes increases the airline's business risks. What drives operational changes, and how much do they affect the airline business?

**Table 2.5      Operational events and cost relationship**

| Disruption events | Delta costs |
| --- | --- |
| Additional flight | Airport, crew, handling, passenger services, route |
| Aircraft change | Airport, crew, revenue loss, route |
| Cancellation | Airport, crew, passenger services, revenue loss, route |
| Aircraft damage | Airport, aircraft repair, crew, passenger services, revenue loss, route, subcharter |
| Delay | Airport, crew, handling, passenger services, route |
| Diversion | Airport, crew, passenger services, revenue loss, route |
| Subchartered aircraft | Aircraft rentals (not separated from commercial rentals) ACMI, wet lease, dry lease |

Most of the time, disruptions are the result of more than one factor, which could occur simultaneously. Some of these factors are obvious, but many of them are not easy to recognise as such – even the experienced managers have difficulties associating them with disrupted operations. The origins of disrupted operations are just partly operational, and are defined by the IATA delay coding system. The majority of them have roots outside of the operational environment, created in various parts of an organisation, and are often of an intangible nature that not many airline managers associate with disruptions. Although it may not be easy to fully understand these reasons and their interconnections, ignoring them and continuing to use a simplistic approach to report on root causes of disruptions can only deepen the disruption problem and will not bring longer lasting improvements.

Despite many airline efforts to monitor delays and the use of various models to simulate operational situations during the planning process, continuous increase in the number of disruptions indicates that current system used to manage disruptions is not sufficiently effective. Among the main system weaknesses is the insufficient knowledge about the root causes and costs of disruptions. In this and in the following chapter we will be looking at the weaknesses of the current system for delay cause monitoring, and find out more about intangible causes of operational disruptions.

Current information about delay reasons is only the visible part of a much wider list of issues describing factors that affect disrupted operations. Reports on operational causes of delays are based on a long established IATA delay coding system. This system includes 100 delay reasons grouped in the following ten major categories (detailed reference to IATA delay codes can be found in Appendix 1):

| Standard IATA Delay Code Groups | |
| --- | --- |
| 0–10 | Free Airline Coding |
| 11–20 | Passenger and Baggage |
| 21–30 | Cargo and Mail |
| 31–40 | Aircraft and Ramp Handling |
| 41–50 | Technical and Aircraft Equipment |
| 51–60 | Damage to Aircraft & EDP/Automated Equipment Failure |
| 61–70 | Flight Operations and Crewing |
| 71–80 | Weather |
| 81–84 | ATFM + Airport + Governmental Authorities, Air Traffic Flow Management Restrictions |
| 85–90 | Airport and Governmental Authorities |
| 91–96 | Reactionary |
| 97–99 | Miscellaneous |

*Note*: Reasons for delays are classified in different ways by Eurocontol and FAA who provide 'translation' tables.

IATA's delay coding system is accepted as an industry standard, and has become an integral part of computerised operations control applications, generators of delay reports. Many airlines have introduced even more layers of subcodes into this system, making it overly complex. Theoretically, having more codes to report on delays can provide more precise information about their causes, but this does not have practical value: operations controllers who are already overloaded with work, need to manually enter this information into the computer system and they typically claim to use only ten out of a hundred-and-something codes. On the other hand, airlines rarely allocate codes for frequent problems like 'interdepartmental communication', which is then assigned to the randomly chosen disruption causes.

The quality of information about delay reasons depends on number of factors, like manual input, communication between participants involved in the disruption process and quality of work procedures. Without good organisation, discipline and control, the reliability of output information will always be questionable and unreliable for decision making at system level.

Current operations control systems do not provide adequate tools for capturing full information about root causes and do not allow for thorough analysis of delays. In addition, untrained staff, and lack of supervision can further decrease reliability of such important business information. Inexperienced operations controllers who are not aware of the real causes of disruptions will feed the system subjectively, register the last most obvious reason of delay, and may not describe adequately what really happened – sometimes they may not describe the event at all due to the lack of time. Many input problems occur during exchange of shifts, when the 'fresh' controller may ignore the sequence of delay causes and assign the initial cause for delay to the latest reactionary flight, as shown in Table 2.6. As a result, the report will be distorted and information about full effects of delays will be forever lost, unless there is an established system for input control from which this information could be recovered. One of the methods some airlines use to overcome this problem is to utilise the existing knowledge of people involved in the key processes around operations soon after the event – they normally know more about the reasons for disruptions than they are ready to formally report.

One of my encounters with the benefits of this method was with an airline suffering from a large number of disruptions, which remained wrongly reported or not reported at all. The root causes of unexpected financial losses were not very clear, but it was obvious that huge losses have been generated during recovery from frequent and long lasting disrupted services. With the support of a disruption monitoring system, it was possible to isolate the most cost critical disruptions over the observed period of time. My attention was drawn to a case where a few days' long disrupted operation resulted in high losses and thousands of disrupted passengers in just a few days. The primary reason was recorded as 'crewing', but there were too many ambiguities and contradictions in the operations report which prompted me to talk to people across the airline that were directly and indirectly involved in this event. They included operations control, flight operations, crew planning, engineering, schedule and network planning, ground operations, reservations, customer services, and senior managers. It did not take me long to compile 'individual truths' and recreate a more objective picture of what has really happened. The root cause shifted a long way from the reported crew problem, back to the network, fleet planning and scheduling issues, and COO responsibilities. During this process, many other problems were discovered, from poor quality of management and ambiguities in internal procedures, to internal communications and information system management.

In organisations that pay little or no attention to the quality of disruption information, things like subjectivity and cultural issues will always, to a more or less degree, affect the reporting on causes of disruptions. It is not surprising that not many airline executives trust delay codes. They know that these reports could be misleading, and hardly make any serious decision based on information contained in delay reports.

Despite management awareness about the weaknesses of the existing system for tracking disruption reasons, they don't do much to make improvements in this area. The existing, seemingly well organised and structured causal system for monitoring delay causes continue to 'steal' management attention, leaving majority of true root causes out of their sight. This 'myopic' perspective only helps disruptions to grow, pushes the costs up, weakens the market position, and allows the managers to call upon complexities and uncertainty to hide inefficiencies.

## Table 2.6    Example of errors in delay reporting

Airline 1

| Airline | DEP | ARR | TAIL No | DEP Delay Min | ARR Delay Min | Reason 1 | Delay 1 | Reason 2 | Delay 2 |
|---|---|---|---|---|---|---|---|---|---|
| Airline 1 | AAA | BBB | A-EATJ | 110 | 100 | 93 | 100 | 87 | 10 |
| Airline 1 | BBB | AAA | A-EATJ | 107 | 105 | | | | |

Initial delay starts with reactionary code. Second flight left without coded reason.

Airline 2

| Airline | DEP | ARR | TAIL No | DEP Delay Min | ARR Delay Min | Reason 1 | Delay 1 | Reason 2 | Delay 2 |
|---|---|---|---|---|---|---|---|---|---|
| Airline 2 | CCC | DDD | B-BEEB | 135 | 120 | 16 | 70 | 81 | 50 |
| Airline 2 | DDD | CCC | B-BEEB | 205 | 202 | | | | |
| Airline 2 | CCC | DDD | B-BEEB | 140 | 145 | 93 | 140 | | |

Reasons for second flight are missing. Not all minutes reported due to a lack of space for more than two reasons.

Airline 3

| Airline | DEP | ARR | TAIL No | DEP Delay Min | ARR Delay Min | Reason 1 | Delay 1 | Reason 2 | Delay 2 |
|---|---|---|---|---|---|---|---|---|---|
| Airline 3 | EEE | FFF | C-AOJE | 30 | 33 | | | | |
| Airline 3 | FFF | GGG | C-AOJE | 26 | 34 | | | | |
| Airline 3 | GGG | FFF | C-AOJE | 59 | 109 | | | | |
| Airline 3 | FFF | HHH | C-AOJE | 107 | 130 | | | | |
| Airline 3 | HHH | FFF | C-AOJE | 335 | 330 | 93 | 335 | | |
| Airline 3 | FFF | EEE | C-AOJE | 57 | 116 | | | | |

Majority of input is missing, only record entered is reactionary.

Industry analysts haven't got much choice but to rely on delay reports provided by various airline organisations, where root cause information becomes even more distorted where root cause information becomes even more distorted. Although this problem has only been publicly acknowledged on a few occasions, it did not prevent information providers from publishing this unreliable information in their official reports. For example, in their Punctuality Performance report for 2007, AEA accepts that 'apportioning delay by reason is an inexact science', but then uses the same information to point out that: 'nevertheless, 42 per cent of primary delays occurred in the pre-flight preparation phase, that is to say, the aircraft was not ready to leave at its departure time, for operational or technical reasons, or because the loading process had not been completed...' The question is how many industry experts really use this information, and if they do, what kind of decisions do they base on this knowledge?

The current situation with a growing number of disruptions and their increasingly costly consequences asks for a change in approach to their management and control. Airline executives need to understand the cross-functional character of underlying operational problems, as this is the only way they could be successfully resolved. Every schedule change caused by crew, maintenance, or any other operational problem, puts other available resources out of balance, and results in flight delays, cancellations and other operational events that are caused by multiple reasons.

Some of the daily situations include the issues like errors in scheduling, crewing, or operations planning, quality of data input, or the lack of disruption related procedures and discipline, that can be easily spotted and eliminated at departmental levels. However, problems related to the more complex situations of strategic nature, with the interference of multiple underlying causes that can have longer and more damaging effects on airline results, require attention of senior managers. They should become involved whenever disruption events cross the critical cost threshold, be able to recognise emerging problems hidden behind highly repetitive patterns, and act before these minor problems reach a tipping point and turn into the more serious issues. Recognising potential loss generators early enough is a key for successful disruption management. The following chapter describes intangible disruption reasons that can support these actions.

# Chapter 3
# Hidden Causes of Operational Disruptions

Despite many efforts to achieve better on-time performance through introduction of costly schedule buffers, fleet renewals, spare aircraft and crew resources, most airlines are still faced with growing disruption problems. Expansion strategies of traditional network carriers to already overcrowded airports and air space are surely among the factors that are diminishing these efforts. AEA reported that 2007 was the fourth successive year with deteriorating punctuality on intra-European flights, adding that figures for June and July, at 29.7 per cent and 28.3 per cent respectively, were the highest individual monthly figures since summer 2000. In the US, 2007 was the year of the industry's second poorest delay performance on record, and analysts say it is likely to get worse. The magnitude of decline in punctuality is shown in Figure 3.1.

Some of the major airports and ATC continue to accommodate the growing traffic in congested areas, despite the fact that they do not have capacities to handle the existing operations. They have become a huge driver of disruptions, with costly knock-on consequences on other parts of the system. As problems with underdeveloped infrastructure will take years to improve, airlines must find other ways to relieve the pressure from congested airports and air routes, and avoid further deterioration in operational and cost effectiveness. In order to create new strategies, they need to better understand the true operational constraints, and how much money they lose by pushing for development over acceptable limits from where their business starts to deteriorate. In this chapter, we will shed more light on the area of usually hidden causes of disruptions of a cross-functional nature. They will reveal a high level of interdependences between internal functions, and can become a valuable source of business information that can help airlines focus on the most critical issues, that spread across the system and have longer lasting effects. These causes are not directly visible – they are indirect and have a relational character. Actions on resolving the problems initiated by these disruption reasons will create bonds between functional areas and strengthen the organisation.

For reasons explained in the previous chapter, the IATA coding system does not provide airlines with complete and reliable information about causes of disruptions. The whole process has to be improved but, more importantly, airline executives need to have a clearer picture about reasons for operational disruptiveness. The majority of disruption risks are rooted more deeply inside the airlines, and increasingly depend on external services provided by airports, ATC and other external sources.

Almost every airline department may hold some responsibility for disruptions, but the majority of them originate in more than one department. In order to

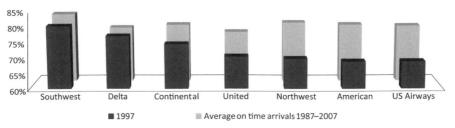

*Source*: US DoT, Air Travel Consumer Report, December 2007

**Figure 3.1    US airline's punctuality comparison, 2007 vs 1987–2007 (on time arrivals)**

allocate the underlying problems more precisely, airlines have to start from tangible information about disruption causes, and then look closely at functions and processes, assess the management and cultural issues, understand external influences, and most importantly, put all this information into a *system* context.

None of the indirect causes of disruptions that will be mentioned here are new to airline professionals. The only novelty is that they will be observed from a different perspective, within the context of disrupted operations. These indirect causes are behind the majority of operational changes, be it insufficient number of pilots to operate an extensive multi-hub network, lack of operational procedures or incompetent management. Until identified and linked with disruptions and cost consequences, they will continue to affect airline operational performance with unknown consequences on financial results and punctuality. Let us look at some of the indirect causes of disruptions. They are grouped in the following four categories:

1. System functions.
2. Management/people/knowledge.
3. Third-party damages and safety.
4. External issues.

**System Functions**

*Strategy*

Disrupted operation is, to a great extent, the result of airline strategies, especially those related to network and fleet structure and investment in people and knowledge. Every change in network or fleet plans, such as expansion to congested airports, introduction of new airport, route or new aircraft type or version, maintenance and crew bases, creates a new opportunity for growth, but increases the level of disruption risks and consequent losses. The tendency of some airlines to satisfy every market segment – long-haul and short-haul, domestic and international, direct and connecting traffic – also increases the risks of disruptions, and operational losses. In addition, the more changes an airline introduces, the bigger the likelihood of things going wrong, especially in organisations with a shortage of experienced people with system knowledge often lost through persistent cuts in labour costs. In big organisations strategists are much more detached from operations – unaligned policies lead to creation of plans that do not match basic operational requirements. They also need more time to adjust to market fluctuations and other strategic changes required to keep them competitive, which create additional strains on the quality of operational and system performance. As a result, deviations from planned operations to a great extent become unavoidable, and come at high costs.

True low-cost carriers like Southwest and Ryanair who operate more simple fleet and root networks from less congested airports, and have less complex organisations, have narrowed the gap between strategic and operations planning and significantly reduced disruption risks and related losses. The results of research carried out by Niehues *et al.* (2001, 3) revealed that there is a correlation between airline punctuality and profitability. Figures comparing operating margin vs. punctuality of major US and European carriers, indicate that despite the statistical limitations of the report, punctual airlines appear to be more profitable. Major airlines with above average on-time performance have been more profitable than those with lower than average punctuality.

Efficient network structure is a foundation for good on-time performance. Both 'hub-and-spoke' and 'point-to-point' network systems play an important role in satisfying customer demand. However, there is a clear distinction in operational efficiency between these two models. Traditional carriers operating 'hub-and-spoke' networks offer passengers the opportunity to travel on more routes and more frequent services. Concentration of operations at peaks in order to provide effective passenger connections creates congestions and longer aircraft ground times. It results in low labour and aircraft utilisation, and a costly system structured around low yield connecting passengers. The fact that these passengers provide 35 to 45 per cent lower revenue per mile than local passengers, and require more complicated logistics, surely raises many questions of a strategic nature (Hasson *et al.*, 2002). Changes in a planned schedule at a hub airport, or even a single route operating from a hub, are frequent and have potential to spread adverse effects widely across the network. Diversified fleet and network structures make scheduling, resource planning processes, and other functions, more complicated, and require lots of knowledge and skills to coordinate them. This also creates problems with information management and leaves airline executives unaware about many critical system issues that often remain unresolved.

The simplicity of the low-cost operating model eliminates much of the above problems. Still, not all low-cost carriers achieve punctuality above industry average. The further away they are from the basic principles of the low cost strategies (point-to-point network, single aircraft type, avoidance of congested airports) the less punctual their operations becomes. The growing category of air carriers that mix the elements of low-cost and traditional operating models known as 'hybrid airlines' generally deliver 'mixed' operational results.

Among factors that could have a negative effect on airline operational performance is the strategy of fast expansion, typical for the new generation of low-cost carriers, necessary to increase their market presence. High growth rates inevitably lead to more complexities and may affect operational performance to a more or less extent. However, in circumstances where punctuality of network carriers continue to deteriorate, the on time performance of true low-cost carriers iz still kept well above the industry averages.

Network airlines have far too many assets to be able to switch quickly some of their operations to a 'depeaked' or 'linear' system as operated by low-cost carriers. Some of them have seen the solution to this problem in formation of 'linear' satellites, operating specialised lean networks.

Whatever the strategy, airlines should be able to look separately at delays inherent in schedule and aircraft rotation plans, and other disruption causes. This is crucial for fine-tuning of network and schedule plans with airline operational capabilities.

During the process of network planning, airlines may not take into account all of the factors that affect the contribution of their major routes to system profitability and on-time performance. Those that do not scrutinise route contribution to system disruptiveness may end up with an 'unknown' increase in costs and reasons of operational disruptions. This especially applies to hub carriers where lack of information about root causes of disruptions at sector level makes it difficult for them to understand the real value of slots held at hub airports, hub operation itself, additional costs, pricing references, loss of revenue and passenger's loyalty.

Let us also mention airline mergers and other types of partnerships when synchronisation of companies' networks and schedules add to increased operational irregularities, and may diminish expected revenue benefits by increased costs of disruptions.

*Scheduling*

Schedule planning is an iterative process that lasts long and requires a variety of skills to balance numerous requirements within and outside the organisation, and resists internal power struggles. As soon as the new seasonal schedule is published, which happens long before the beginning of season, it starts to change. Every schedule change affects a part of the system and may increase disruption risks. Sometimes, airlines even make substantial scheduled changes after the season starts, realising only too late that they failed to recognise the magnitude of operational constraints. This was the case with a major European carrier that had to cancel 10 per cent of their operations in the middle of summer season, due to planning omissions. Another carrier decided to reduce its flying programme by 2 per cent, cancelling 966 scheduled flights 'to protect its operational performance', which happened just two months before the beginning of a new winter season. The move followed a week of continuous flight cancellations because of staff shortages and technical problems at its base airport at the end of the summer schedule.

Among many factors that could be used to measure effectiveness of airline schedules and network efficiency in general is the number and length of schedule buffers. There is no 'standard' scheduled time between two airports. Airlines decide how long it will take depending on the season, time of the day, marketing and slot strategy, and a number of other factors. It varies from airline to airline, and depends on the quality of information. Airlines are forced to extend scheduled times at busy routes and airports knowing that the system will often not allow shortest routings, will involve ATC holdings, flight slow-downs, or idle ground times. As a consequence, most flights are 'delayed' even when they arrive on time, because the way the air transport system works does not allow them to fly as efficiently as they can. Take an example of short-haul flights between London Heathrow and Paris Charles de Gaulle. While navigation flight times between the two airports take no longer than 40 minutes, published schedule times that include buffers vary between 75 and 85 minutes.

Among the scarce statistical reports about the system cost of schedule buffers, Eurocontrol's Performance Review Report (April 2005), claims that 'the cost of one minute of buffer time for an A320 is estimated at €49 per flight. Cutting five minutes on average of 50 per cent of schedules thanks to higher predictability would be worth some €1,000 million per annum, through savings or better use of airline and airport resources.' There are indications that this cost can be much higher for individual airlines, bearing in mind wider aspects of the problem that spreads beyond measurable values.

How effective are the costly 'padded' schedules? There is a practical limit to the amount of expected delays that can be absorbed by flight schedules – padded schedules set higher limits to other operational parameters like aircraft utilisation, crew productivity and aircraft maintenance slots. Increasing block times to accommodate delays can itself cause problems of early arrivals and loss of competitiveness. Eurocontrol statistics show that about a third of flights in Europe landed before scheduled times, and 13 per cent of flights departed before their schedule times in 2006. Punctuality reports indicate that the number of delayed flights operated on highly 'padded' routes may increase, such as happened at Heathrow and JFK airports in the peak summer period of 2007. Inefficient buffers on short-haul routes are occupying too much of valuable aircraft time, which could be more effectively used elsewhere. The block time buffer on the route between London Heathrow and Paris Charles de Gaulle, for example, takes an additional five hours of aircraft utilisation each day. If it were a Ryanair-type airline, it would make up to six additional sectors a day, because it would avoid congested airports like Heathrow and Charles de Gaulle, and its costs would be much lower. The knowledge about true effectiveness of schedule buffers could add a new dimension in quality of strategic decisions as well as network and fleet planning. It could be supported by better understanding of causes and costs of operational disruptions.

*Aircraft related issues*

Fleet composition is, after network structure, the second main influencer of flight irregularities. Airlines that operate a mixed fleet are traditionally hub operators exposed to a higher number and more costly disruptions than airlines with a simpler fleet and networks. In combination with other 'disruption-generating' factors, like multiple technical and crew bases, they can hardly sustain the competition of airlines with more simple operating models.

Fleet utilisation has a direct impact on frequency and volume of flight disruptions. Tight aircraft rotation plans, with too little space for regular maintenance checks and unrealistic turn-around times, are more prone to the cascading effects of initial flight disruptions and take longer to resolve. On the other side, unutilised schedule buffers at congested airports only contribute to overall inefficiencies as they decrease aircraft utilisation.

Airlines may deploy spare aircraft capacities in attempt to improve punctuality. These are costly solutions that could help alleviate some of the disruption problems, but can also become a huge loss maker unless well justified, operationally and financially. There are many examples where airlines deploy reserve aircraft that is later mainly used as a buffer for unscheduled maintenance requirements, with little space left to improve punctuality. Even if it is available, a spare aircraft is sometimes unusable if it cannot operate to a particular airport or route due to performance limitations, and some other restrictions, or if there is no spare crew.

Maintenance-related disruptions are among the most costly causes of disruptions – aircraft taken out of service for unscheduled repairs often take time and spread disruptions throughout the network. Maintenance reliability is pretty much determined by airline strategy, the number of base airports, network and fleet structure, and is affected by the level of synchronisation of operational processes.

Unscheduled maintenance is one of the major causes of operational disruptions, especially with hub-and-spoke operators and airlines with aged fleet. Delta's Managing Director of Maintenance, Repair and Overhaul Process and Technology said that approximately 60 per cent of Delta's maintenance was unplanned in 2003; a statistic that is common in the industry (Brown, 2003). The average cost of having planes idle during unplanned maintenance is around $23,000 per hour, say industry analysts.

Spare part policies are an important determinant of operational disruptiveness. Major US airlines may have $1 billion worth of inventory at any one time. Extreme financial pressure has forced airlines to direct money tied up in inventory to where it is more needed, which has affected the quality and cost of airline operations. It is expected that more accurate forecasting capabilities to predict with greater accuracy when an aircraft is going to be available for maintenance, will mitigate the risk that a reduced stock of spare parts may have on scheduling, aircraft availability, and its utilisation.

*Operational decisions*

Every day airlines make operational changes worth tens, or hundreds of millions in costs, depending on airline size and operating model. Despite such a high level of costs involved in operational changes, decisions are made without much consideration of the cost. Operational decision makers are often faced with dilemmas whether to delay or cancel the flight, reposition or subcharter the aircraft, among many others. Their decisions depend on the quality of information that comes from various sources. Often, it does not come at the time when needed, or may not be available at all. In addition, the large amount of operational information needed to resolve the problem, makes it impossible for operations controllers to more realistically estimate the cost effectiveness of their decisions. The attention of the decision-makers remains predominantly focused on speedy schedule recovery, often leaving them unaware about the consequences their decisions have on other flights, system resources, cost and revenue.

The following examples illustrate some of the situations faced by an operations department during the process of schedule recovery.

It is not uncommon in a busy operational environment where staffing is critical, that an inexperienced controller is put in a position to make decisions with higher risk consequences. An operational 'apprentice' of a young low-fare airline was given the authority to make schedule recovery decisions. Left on his own, without clear instructions, he kept postponing his decisions whenever the situation became complex, waiting for the direction from senior managers, rarely available at the time. Worrying about the unpleasant consequences of making the wrong decisions, he would wait until the operational situation became so critical that flight cancellations and aircraft hiring would remain the only options. It took several months before the consequences of these practices were noticed, incurring hundreds of thousands of dollars in losses in the meantime.

Or, take the case in which an indecisiveness in making operational decision following aircraft damage at an outstation on a long-haul route, caused a 24-hour long delay for the majority of over 300 passengers and a series of long delays affected passengers on reactionary flights during the next two days. The costs were estimated at €750,000, including aircraft repair, passenger accommodation, additional costs for passengers sent to other carriers, technical positioning, replacement aircraft for the remaining passengers, subchartered flight for spare parts, aircraft repositioning, and two days' long knock-on effects on other flights. This was the most costly of several other alternative solutions.

Disruption situations can be extremely complex and difficult to resolve. Among the most challenging ones are those caused by technical problems. Most of the difficulties arise from inability of decision makers to accurately predict how much time it will take to repair the aircraft and, consequently, make operational decisions. One of cases from real life that illustrates uncertainties related to the process of decision making is shown in Appendix 2.

*Crew planning*

A global shortage of pilots has become a big industry problem and is responsible for a significant number of flight disruptions. In these circumstances, airline executives that are faced with challenges to align expansion strategies with crew availability, may try to resolve the problem by increasing the crew operating hours close to the legal maximum, without being aware about the full effects of decision on punctuality and regularity of airline operations. On the other hand, unforeseen schedule changes caused by other interrelated problems, put additional strain on crew planners to make the system work efficiently. As a result, errors during the planning process are not uncommon, and contribute further to a higher number of operational disruptions.

*Sales and marketing*

An airline's place in the global distribution systems (GDS) is one of the enhancers of yield and revenue. The closer they are to the top of the display, the better is their competitive position. In order to reach this position, marketing and sales executives insist on operations at peak times, with short connecting times and tight block times – factors responsible for number of disruption problems, and may become counter-productive to revenue maximization in the long run.

Another source of sales-induced disruptions relates to sales objectives and the way airlines measure individual performance of the sales staff. In airlines with sales-dominated strategies, sales units tend to push for more flights or new routes in order to increase revenue and achieve personal rewards, often with little regard to cost consequences. In order to justify their case more strongly, they may overestimate revenue or unknowingly overlook aircraft-specific restrictions that may incur additional route costs, like limited hold space on routes where passengers carry an excessive amount of baggage, or flying to a destination that cannot be reached without a technical stop. Although these extreme cases are rare, they increase the risk of operational losses with longer term consequences.

The following anecdote illustrates one such case:

> An airline sales executive sold a flight to carry a high profile symphonic orchestra, without considering aircraft limitations. Shortly before the departure date, it was discovered that not all of the instruments could fit into the baggage holds, resulting in flight cancellation, a great inconvenience to the orchestra and leaving the airline with unsold capacities. The airline later received a complaint from the orchestra director with a cynical note, that the only way that the airline sales team would see them again would be as an audience during their concert – but not as returning passengers.

*Investment decisions*

Typically, airlines do not invest enough money and management time in improvements that lead to better operational performance. This is mainly because of insufficient information about the magnitude of the costs involved in disrupted services and their underlying causes. Among many dilemmas faced by senior managers during the decision-making processes is how much (if at all) the company needs to invest in spare aircraft and crew, in information systems, or other critical areas that may increase the risk of disruption losses. Without making targeted investments based on knowledge about main operational constraints, operational problems will continue to accumulate and may generate even higher losses.

Apart from internal investments, effectiveness of airline operation is highly dependent on synchronised development of airport and ATC infrastructure as well as suppliers' investments in equipment, people and training. Current underinvestment in this area causes an increase in the number of disruptions and puts more strain on airlines and passengers.

*Outsourcing*

The continuing trend in outsourcing of non-core activities increases airlines' dependency on external service providers. By contracting out some of their services, airlines are shifting a part of their responsibility for service delivery to external suppliers, and expect to make substantial savings. In reality, however, these advantages could be lessened by additional, uncalculated, often unrecognised disruption losses. Outsourced services could be a source of many hidden operating costs.

A good relationship between airlines and suppliers is vital for on-time performance. Very often, however, things do not go as desired. Airlines and service suppliers have different criteria to measure performance, which may becomes a cause of disputes, and cause deterioration in airline's performance. Other difficulties could arise in situations when an airline does not have a system for monitoring the quality of services provided by third parties.

Period of adjustments to newly outsourced services is typically associated with operational difficulties, and increased number of operational disruptions. Lufthansa's experience was no different, but shows how a series of initial problems could be successfully resolved. Lufthansa and Lufthansa Technique were legally separated in 1995 (Flint, 2001). The separation altered their working relationship to an extent neither side recognised. The staff on both sides became hostile towards each other and even stopped talking. They were both independent profit centres, tending to focus on their own interests, instead of on the overall service product that was delivered to their customers. In over four years, they drifted apart so much that side effects became clearly visible. Deterioration in operational performance was significant, especially at its Frankfurt hub, where punctuality fell into the low 70 per cent. The situation was not resolved before a neutral third party was brought in to work with both sides to address the communication issues, build a framework for the future, and create a common measure for maintenance performance. The process was not easy and came at high price, as Lufthansa had to pool several aircraft out of service for use as spares to improve reliability. The efforts however resulted in significant improvements in on-time performance, with punctuality back up in the 80 per cent range in 2000 leaving the airline to continue to improve punctuality while at the same time decreasing the number of spare aircraft.

There are many other examples of difficulties in dealing with service suppliers whose priorities and interests do not match airline's particular needs, especially if there are ambiguities in their contractual obligations. Airlines that do not put enough efforts into creating a good relationship with their suppliers, and do not have a good system in place to control the quality of this services typically end up with more costly and less punctual operation..

*Software issues*

Errors in software designs are not a rare cause of airline disruptions. There are many examples of massive losses caused by software failures around the industry. In the summer of 2003 US Airways' pilots union blamed management for what it termed an incorrect pilot staffing model, resulting in numerous flight cancellations over several months and affecting thousands of passengers. On the worst day, the airline cancelled 80 flights. In the UK, after the introduction of a new air traffic control system, computer failure caused fleet grounding across the country on several occasions, and affected tens of thousands of passengers.

Other software problems include optimisation tools for crew planning, which have recently become one of the most feared causes of disruptions among airlines. A big European airline was hit hard during the implementation of a new crewing system, resulting in massive disruptions and downsizing of planned traffic. On the less obvious side, the lack of transparency of criteria built into the optimisation software may generate hidden losses in situations that do not ideally match the pre-set optimisation rules. This explains the reluctance of experienced staff to use these tools during the important and time critical decision making. Less experienced staff use them more willingly, but this may later come at a higher cost through the increase in the number of disrupted services.

While some of the consequences of software-related problems might be obvious, others could be more subtle and hard to discover like in the case of poorly trained users.

Many more, often unrecognised, software-related issues, be it schedule, crew or operations planning applications, are causing instability in airline schedules and consequently an increase in operating costs.

Choosing a vendor and a software solution that best fits airlines' requirements is a long and laborious process, during which airlines appear to be in a less favourable position. Firstly, during the purchasing process, they are not able to compare objectively functionalities, prices, and quality of technical support for the competitive products. Secondly, it is not possible for them to properly test the software before it is purchased. The risk of failing to choose the right product increases for those more influenced by a vendor's persuasive abilities, pricing tactics, or other business interests.

Once software is purchased and installed, more often than not, a chain of unpredicted events and associated costs starts to unfold – from problems of a technical and functional nature, through suddenly discovered weaknesses of the internal IT support system, to organisational and procedural issues. Resolving these issues always takes time, during which period the work processes become disturbed, accumulating unforeseen costs hidden behind the rigidity of traditional costing systems.

Most often than not, the agreed package price does not include a sufficient number of training hours. As a result, applications are often misused or are not used to their full potential, resulting in errors, with implications on airline operations.

Apart from slowing down the work processes, low software reliability in combination with poor technical support have caused many costly disruptions that have rarely been identified as the reason for operational disruptions.

The time required and costs involved in airline report customisation are often so high that airline executives rarely approve additional investments. The choice of standard reports has always been a disputable issue between airlines and vendors. As a consequence, the lack of valuable planning and operational information can cause additional operational problems and leave senior executives out of touch with reality. Introduction of flexible reporting systems and business intelligence tools has only partly resolved these issues, as they require users with advanced knowledge and skills that are not always available.

## Managing/People/Knowledge

### *Management time*

In absence of reliable information for disruption management, senior executives may spend too much of their valuable time trying to understand and even resolve the daily problems that could be managed at operational level. Apart from interfering in decision making in the area where their competence may be questionable, they are missing the opportunity to focus on more important issues, which may remain unresolved and affect operational results.

### *Fast decision making*

The myth of modern organisations that it is better to make a bad decision than no decision could be dangerous especially in situations when the issues are not clear, data is unreliable, and the context is unstructured, which is the case with disruptions related decisions. Management response to unknown problems has significant impact on the quality of decision making – operational, as well as strategic. The reactions in these situations could be very different – from delegating the task up or down, procrastinating by waiting for 'more details' or making the decision too quickly and then, if at all possible, modifying it. The chances are that they would open up new problems with, often, hidden, undesired losses.

Generally, the popular practice of fast decision making may be highly beneficial when it is supported with knowledge, experience and based on reliable hard information. As this is not always the case in airline practices, many short- and even long-term decisions made at higher organisational levels cause operational and financial problems, and become hidden causes of operational disruptions. One of these cases is described in the following example.

A charismatic leader of a young low cost airline built himself a reputation as a 'fast decision maker', never allowing 'paralysis by analysis', which made him very efficient in many situations. However, problems started to emerge when the speed of decision making began to dominate over the clear and solid strategic visions. The basics of low cost principles were soon replaced with trial and error approach to almost every area of business strategy, from network and fleet structures to marketing. The decisions to introduce new routes and new airports into the airline's scheduled services were made fast, as were the decisions to pool out from the route after several months of unsuccessful operation. When it became obvious that these 'strategies' did not work, the airline turned to a seemingly more lucrative business, wet-leasing a part of its fleet to carriers located at airports away from the airline's technical and crew bases. In haste to secure the business, the airline failed to take into account the cost and consequences of aircraft and crew positioning, as well as the effects of this new venture on its own resources. The fulfilment of contractual obligations towards operating partner created shortages in aircraft and crew capacities, and seriously affected airlines' own operational performance. The 'unexpected' events started to accumulate, and incurred losses became much higher than the airline had ever anticipated.

*Imbalance in management power*

Inside each airline, many unrecognised power chains can directly or indirectly influence decisions related to operational disruptions. They involve powerful individuals, departments or other informal sources within and outside the organisation. Their narrow interests can create many operational problems, affecting cost and revenue. Among them is the traditional power struggle between marketing and sales functions on one side and operations on another. If these two functions are not well balanced during the planning process, they can create the problems at a later stage: if a market-driven strategy prevails by exceeding operational capabilities, there will be more disruptions and costs will be higher; while if operational interests take a stronger stand, they can affect airline sales strategies and eventually result in less revenue.

## Knowledge and people

Airlines are under constant pressure to cut costs and increase profit, even if they already operate profitably. Those that have exploited the majority of cost-saving measures, and need to make further reductions, find it difficult to 'invent' a new set of measures which will make the airline more profitable in the quickest possible way. Senior managers then take the easiest 'escape route' and turn to labour cost cutting, with little awareness or concern about how much value competent people bring to the organisation. Every time people leave the company, there is a break in knowledge transfer. The cuts in labour cost over a number of years have pushed some airlines into serious problems. While their profit margins may still look good for reasons other than the core business, lack of care for the airline's longer term interests and incompetence could be recognised through the growing number and length of costly operational disruptions.

In some companies, inexperienced and insufficiently trained operations staff are often given the authority to make cost-sensitive decisions far too soon. The wrong choice of solution to operational problems, where decision makers are faced with dilemmas whether to delay, divert or cancel flights, substitute, rent or reposition the aircraft, without understanding the wider consequences of each of these decisions may incur millions of dollars in losses over just one year, can increase losses. The paradox is that no matter how many unnecessary losses were generated during operational decision making, operations staff can still be rewarded if, typically, their personal performance is measured by the increase in overall punctuality. A similar situation applies to people involved in other activities that have an indirect impact on operational performance. In absence of clear directions and supervision, the knowledge-related problems will remain unnoticed, often hidden behind departmental walls, and continue to disrupt the operations.

Another area where lack of system knowledge can directly affect planned operations is aircraft purchasing and implementation. It is not rare that some aspects of aircraft operational capabilities and performance are overlooked during the contract negotiations, making it impossible for aircraft to operate on some of the planned routes. These problems are often discovered too late to avoid delays, technical stops and cancellations, and cause changes in schedule and in annual plans. The process of implementation of new aircraft does not happen all that often, but it is always linked with an increased number of operational disruptions.

Many airlines have willingly decided not to keep 'costly knowledge workers' on their payroll, and have found it more cost effective to occasionally hire specialists to carry out the required work. It is very important for airlines to distinguish which kind of work should be bought in, in order to avoid unnecessary investments in jobs that sometimes not only do not deliver expected longer term results, but are also demotivating for airline staff. An airline must predominantly rely on its internal workforce, who has the necessary motivation to deliver longer lasting results. However, things become harder if a company lacks experienced people with *system* knowledge, who may have been lost because of relentless 'labour' cuts, and thereby carrying out a part of the knowledge of their organisations. Henry Mintzberg explains: 'Sure, there was useful information in the computers – explicit information. But far more important was the tacit information contained in the heads of the experienced people, and no corporation had the program to download that' (Mintzberg, 2006).

Air carriers that have enjoyed longer lasting success do rely on their own knowledgeable workforce. What a consultant can do is to inspire, and say some useful things that, in combination with management knowledge about the context, may lead to better solutions. Understanding disruptions means living with them and learning from them continually, not just until the new consulting project ends.

*Cost cutting measures*

It is an embodied belief that airlines can meet their objectives only if they cut costs. It is always good to do it for less, no matter how well the airline performed financially. When dealing with measurable costs, this is fine. The costs, however, also control things that are less open to financial measurement, like quality of service, safety, and knowledge, or treatment of employees. Even if they cannot be measured, they define the future state of the business and may be more important for the airline than current financial results. Cutting the labour costs can show more profit but, without good consideration of the full consequences, it can bring the organisation into financial crisis as soon as the next year. Investing in training and improvements in information systems, for example, may appear as a cost burden in this year's budget plan, but there is a good chance that it will bring more success in the next year and the following years. All of these factors directly relate to the quality of airline planning, management and control and consequently reflect on the number and type of operational disruptions.

*Punctuality targets*

In order to make a good estimate about the punctuality targets, airline executives need to understand the system limitations, which is the key for successful operations planning. Setting the targets right requires wide knowledge of interrelated processes, operational dynamics and solid disruption risk evaluation. If an airline introduces spare capacities or hires additional crew to ease the disruption problems, this does not mean that it should automatically increase the punctuality targets. It may appear that keeping the target at the same level as the previous year is more realistic, leaving some space for additional, sometimes even predictable constraints like limitations of airport capacities, strike actions or new security measures. Investment in punctuality may improve the on-time performance, but make the airline less profitable due to high punctuality costs.

Realistically set punctuality targets play an important role in staff motivation. Targets that are set too high could have a negative impact on airline staff. For those who work hard to avoid delays, while the outcome is always below their expectations, this may be quite disappointing, especially if their personal rewards depend on the overall on-time performance.

Setting the targets too low is equally bad and demotivates people involved in planning and operations processes. Only a good understanding of internal and external constraints, their frequency, intensity, length, trends, and influence on airline costs and revenue can help the airline to set them more realistically. There are cases in airline practices when top executives, who are detached from operational problems, unilaterally decide to introduce 'new measures' to improve punctuality, adding even more confusion to already complex problems, such as in the following case.

Concerned about months' long decline of already poor on-time performance, and pressure to do something about it, a newly promoted senior executive of a medium-size airline 'commanded' during the management meeting that no flight delay should be tolerated unless really critical. 'Does that mean that when faced with options for the flight to leave on-time by using a longer route and burn more fuel, or depart 15–20 minutes later in order to operate a 30 minutes shorter route, we should still opt for an on-time departure?' asked Operations Manager. Sensible question was followed by sensible reply: 'Well,' said the executive, 'we really need to take a closer look at this problem ...' As this discussion did not continue and did not trigger further actions on improvements in on-time performance, there were no changes in the existing practices and, consequently, no improvements in punctuality.

## Cross-functional communication

One of the greatest obstacles in communicating change messages across the organisation is airline departmental detachment. Airline activities are traditionally divided and subdivided in discrete departmental tasks so that individual tasks could be more closely monitored, measured, and 'fine-tuned' to produce the most efficient performance from each activity. These functional separations and individual measures of performance, however, have generated many problems related to operational and cost efficiency.

Operational decision makers often complain that they are not given instructions about cost elements and commercial priorities necessary for efficient decision making, and are left to rely on their subjective judgements. On the other side, network and strategic planners are overloaded with the number of factors they need to compromise on in order to optimise the system plan. They sometimes do not pay much attention to operational limitations and suggestions that they do not consider as 'critical'. As a result, the ignored 'minor' problems may soon start to accumulate and more seriously disrupt the operations. It can create costly cascading effects, like in the situations when insufficient time is left for technical checks, or when evening flights to airports with night curfews are planned to operate at the end of aircraft rotation, which in both cases can develop into a frequent, lengthy, and costly disruptions.

Disputes between different departments and layers of management, especially those long standing, can seriously affect operational stability and are not easy to identify and resolve. Difficulties in communication between strategic and scheduling departments, and scheduling and operations are almost proverbial. A big charter airline addressed the problem by inviting an external consultant to arrange and chair the meeting between heads of operations and scheduling departments who refused to communicate with each other, and help them to resolve the issues which they were failing to discuss and reach agreement on. In many airlines, however, these problems may pass unnoticed by senior management, despite the fact that they have direct implications on operational and financial performance.

These kind of problems are, to a great extent, created by different objectives that each of the departments need to meet during the planning process. For example, while network and schedule planners tend to maximise aircraft utilisation and revenue potential, maintenance and operations planners will ask for looser aircraft rotation in order to get much needed space so they can cope more successfully with disrupted operations. If these two objectives are not well synchronised with ultimate system goals, the result could be lower aircraft utilisation with less revenue opportunities, or an increased number of 'unexpected' disruptions. The trade-off between the wide variety of requirements, needs to be transparent, with clearly set objectives, and whenever possible based on reliable hard information. Cross-functional activities of this kind require involvement of airline leaders, who should ensure that people are not confused about the main airline values, and understand how much they can benefit from well-synchronised activities at *system* level.

*Airline culture*

Airline culture is a reflection of the collective attitudes and behaviour of employees towards the way they do their jobs, communicate across functional lines, express new ideas or concerns, work with managers, and vice versa, use and share what they know and how they relate to customers and service suppliers. It is very much influenced by the way individual performance is measured and rewarded, the level of their job security, and opportunities for learning. It also depends on a free flow of information not only within an organisation, but also between airline and many external stakeholders, including the public.

Organisational effectiveness depends on the healthy flow of information which affects its capacity to solve problems, innovate, meet challenges, and compete. That flow may be blocked especially in situations when the disruption information reveals facts that can hardly be accepted at senior level management levels.

This kind of culture is a stumbling block to improvements in airline operational efficiency, as systematic flaws in information flow are just postponing their damage for another day. If people have a fear of reporting errors, bringing bad news, or being blamed for mistakes, they may induce losses that are difficult to discover and quantify.

Introduction of principles for disruption management, which should be at the core of quality improvement, assumes cultural changes. One of the reasons why many disruption or delay management programmes fail is because they were run as 'programmes' and not ingrained in the overall business model and company strategies. The sustained success of Southwest Airlines, for example, was based on the company's culture that places a heavy emphasis on the collaboration and teamwork of a strong and stable workforce. It has integrated the importance of quality in its overall business model, strategic plan and its daily operational activities. They did not engage outside consultants to develop temporary 'quality programmes', but rather its style, culture, and emphasis on quality were implemented in Southwest's daily activities by the airline's leader and his management team.

Quality, accessibility, and share of business information could significantly shape organisational culture and affect the quality of management decisions. This has been confirmed by findings based on survey conducted in 2004 by YouGov, a high-profile British Internet-based opinion pollster, which shows that firms often fail to provide the right information to enable staff to do their jobs properly and impose unreasonable deadlines. According to the survey, almost two-thirds of people blamed a lack of information for their 'blagging' to bosses and almost a quarter were not sure that the information they were expected to act upon was correct. This decreases the likelihood that decisions made at the top of chain will work best for the organisation.

There are various business issues that can affect staff morale with an, often unknown, impact on quality and cost of airline operation. Among them are the management practices based on hidden agendas, as was the case of a major airline, which organised a three months long cost-saving project involving people from every corner of the organisation. As it was later discovered, the main objective of the project was not to save costs at 'every corner of the airline', but to cut a predetermined number of middle managers. This revelation has started to create a distrust in the management team, which continued with similar practices, contributing to a longer term decline in airline overall results, including deterioration in operational performance. This real life story is described in Appendix 4.


**Third Party Damages and Safety**

*Damages caused by third parties*

Airline service providers (ATC, ground handling companies, manufacturers, technology service providers), may generate massive disruptions of airline schedules and incur significant losses. Lack of reliable information and management awareness about the full scale of these damages often prevents airlines from claiming compensations and investing in their prevention. Aircraft damages at congested airports are among the most frequent and most costly ones. The problems are exacerbated by handling companies which, in order to save costs, tend to underinvest in staff and their training, and postpone investment in necessary equipment.

*Safety*

Operational disruptions increase the risks of incidents and accidents, particularly at congested airports, where this exposure is higher and often result in aircraft damages and other ramp handling incidents. They also affect flight crews – there is evidence of a direct relationship between the length of time spent on duty and the increase in safety-related incidents. Any disruption to the planned crew roster may have an effect on the level of fatigue suffered by individual pilots. Disruptions are far more likely to occur in those companies with minimum staffing levels, and where the ratio of crews per aircraft falls short of the optimum for the route structure. In such situations, airlines could push available pilots to fly right up to the legal limits in order to keep flights operating on time.

**External Issues**

*Airport and ATC capacities*

The level of traffic congestion on many major routes and at biggest airports has reached a stage where a further increase in traffic can have a serious impact on airline passengers and safety. According to FAA, arrival delays at JFK were increased for 114 per cent in the first ten months of the fiscal year 2007, with on-time performance of just 59 per cent in June and July. The daily average number of delays, which rose to 50 a day between 2000 and 2006, rocketed to 102 a day in the financial year 2007. In addition, the daily number of taxi times that took longer than an hour averaged 51, twice that of 2006 (*Airport International* March 2008).

The main cause for such a serious shortage of capacities is the 'hub-and-spoke' network model, which has forced concentration of traffic to just a few airports. Over half of the total US air traffic is routed through only 17 out of 422 airports capable of handling landings, take-offs and service of commercial air flights. Delays initiated at JFK airport alone create 50 per cent of reactionary delays in the US. In addition, a report published by JEC (US Joint Economic Committee 2008, 2), revealed that delays involving flights to and from the 35 largest US airports accounted for about half of the total passenger delays in 2007.

A similar situation holds in Europe, where European airports generally have too much capacity or too much traffic. The future does not look bright. Eurocontrol points out that 'airports are constrained in their ability to produce this capacity by physical site and infrastructure limitations, environmental issues and physical constraints related to surrounding airspace and geography'. The following figures illustrate the severity of problem which could have a long-term implications on the entire air transport system:

- Of 130 operating airlines, a network of over 450 airports and some 60 air navigation services providers, only 1.5 per cent of city pairs in Europe carry 75 per cent of passenger seats (European Commission, November 2000, Consultation Paper on a Community Air Passenger Report on Service Quality Indicators).
- 16 congested airports generate 80 per cent of EU delays (AEA).
- The proportion of air-traffic delays that occurs at airports (as opposed to en route) doubled from 23 per cent in 2000 to 46 per cent three years later (Eurocontrol).
- Even if the capacity of the airport network increases by 60 per cent, by 2025, a potential 3.7 million flights per annum will not be accommodated. As a result, more than 60 airports will be congested and the top 20 European airports will be saturated at least eight to ten hours a day. This is explained by the fact that 75 per cent of European airports see no possibility for building new runways in the next 20 years (Eurocontrol, January 2006).
- The distribution of world airport traffic is uneven – 82 per cent of passenger traffic worldwide is carried through just 18 per cent of airports with over 2.3 billion passengers annually (IATA, 2006).

Consequences of disruptions on passengers travelling through congested airports should be taken more seriously. They make flying less attractive, more expensive and a cause of frustration, anxiety, and inconvenience for passengers. The magnitude of losses for airports and airlines could be vast if problems at congested airports get worse.

The situation is not much better with airspace congestion, which is the most frequent single reason for flight delays. Eurocontrol PRR (Performance Review Commission Report) 2006 noted that each aircraft flies an average of 48.6 km more than necessary due to the structure and use of en route airspace (5.9 per cent of average distance flown); in other words, additional 467 million kilometres, or 11,664 flights around the world. To improve corresponding environmental and financial impacts, the Eurocontrol Council adopted a target to reduce the additional distance flown by 220 million km between 2007 and 2010 – the equivalent of removing 24,000 flights from the European airspace system in a year. The Council expects to save 1 billion Euros and reduce $CO_2$ emission by 2.3 million tonnes.

*Ground services*

Increased airline competition has caused shortening of aircraft ground times, resulting in additional pressure on ground personnel and higher risk of delays. Growing competitiveness of ramp handling service providers has contributed to a cut in labour costs and underinvestment in equipment and training with consequences on the quality of ground services and safety.

*Aeronautical information*

The comprehensive and sometimes inadequate systems for publication of aeronautical information about status of navigation facilities, procedures, services and airports and the way they are handled by airlines is a frequent cause of disruptions. Too often, airlines and pilots are informed about changes, or temporary airport restrictions when it is too late, or do not receive this information at all, incurring high costs of rescheduling, diversions and even flight cancellations, with implications on safety.

*Effects of airline disruptions on service providers*

Airlines themselves can cause disruptions to their service providers. The majority of problems arise from unrealistic schedules because of the lack of slots or the desire to show better connectivity through reservation systems. Unworkable block and aircraft turn times affect the operation of other service providers such as airports, ATC, handling companies and so on, who then become a new source of disruptions, causing further delays that may spread to other airlines and across other networks.

Airports view delays from a different perspective. Apart from problems experienced by unrealistic airline schedules, their difficulties to keep punctuality high, often arise from many other factors. They include: uneven schedule distribution; arrival/departure priority; environmental or weather constraints; congestion in the terminal building, ramp area or on taxiways, and can also be caused by non-local airport factors like congestion or bad weather at other airports, when aircraft may be held on the ground because of congestion at the destination airport, to avoid airborne holding en route or in the terminal area. Congestion may occur because airports allow an excessive number of landings and take-offs, and airlines add flights without giving enough consideration to the fact that their operations will be delayed and will cause a rippling effect on their own flights as well as on other carriers. Despite obvious problems, airlines continue to increase their traffic at highly overstretched airports like Heathrow, where almost 40 per cent of flights in 2007 were delayed for more than 15 minutes and an average flight was delayed for 20 minutes. The decline in punctuality at Heathrow airport between 2002 and 2007 is shown in Figure 3.2.

*Taxi-out delays*

According to US statistics, 40 per cent of delays in the year 2000 occurred while the aircraft moved from the gate to the runway. The high frequency of taxi-out delays (nearly 10 minutes each), resulted in about a half of the total delay time being accumulated in that category. Since the FAA does not begin counting delays until more than 14 minutes have elapsed, its system does not capture many taxiing and airborne delays. The rise in ground-based delays could be partly explained by

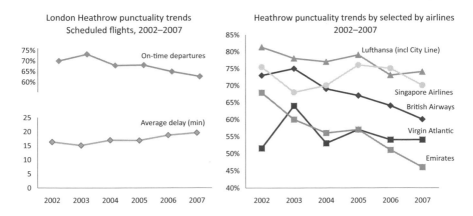

**Figure 3.2    Punctuality trends at Heathrow airport (total scheduled operations and by selected airlines) 2002–2007**

*Source*: www.flightontime.info

the action of aviation authorities who more frequently have imposed ground stops to increase space between aircraft in the air. Furthermore, limited terminal spaces at major airports made it necessary to clear the gate and incur a delay in the taxi-out phase of flight so as not to impede inbound traffic.

The processes of flight departures and arrivals involve three tightly connected segments owned by airlines, airports, and air traffic control. While their individual accountability is officially regulated, there are many loose or even non-existent links between them, increasing the risk of flight disruptions. The problem with airlines is that they typically do not have the processes and systems in place to monitor the performance of handling agents, causing the rise in often wrongly allocated disruptions.

*Regulatory issues*

The continuous increase in the number and duration of flight delays, together with the rising volume of cancelled flights, are causing growing passenger dissatisfaction. In the US, it has reached the stage where it has become necessary for the government to become involved. After a series of extreme disruption incidents at US airports in 2006 and 2007, the government had to intervene to protect the interests of air passengers by ordering airlines to enter a voluntary agreement to reduce peak operation at the worst affected airport – JFK. The US Transportation Secretary even warned that the alternative might be to 'return to the days of government-regulated flights and limited competition'. After a month's long process that involved major US airlines serving JFK, together with airports and consumer advocates, a formal agreement to cap hourly operations at one of the world's busiest airports was reached.

*Coordination at industry level*

Many disruptions are caused by failure of policy makers to provide synchronised development and control of air transport facilities and resources. Collaborative decision making at this level has a particular role to play, allowing informed decisions to be made in real time, in response to rapidly changing conditions. This is of particular importance for areas with congested airports and airspace, which bear responsibility for a great majority of flight delays and higher costs of airline operations.

We have so far set the framework for disruption cause analysis in the belief that problems are best solved by attempting to correct or eliminate root causes, as opposed to merely addressing the immediately obvious symptoms. The next step is to devise a way of integrating the knowledge about direct and indirect causes of disruptions into a single disruption management system that will support discovery of problem areas, root causes and their order of magnitude. By directing corrective measures at root causes, it is hoped that the likelihood of problems recurring will be minimised. However, it is recognised that complete prevention of recurrence by a single intervention is not always possible. Thus, root cause analysis is often considered an iterative process, and is frequently viewed as a tool of continuous improvement.

# Chapter 4
# Organising Disruption Information

So far we have described the disruption problem across the industry, and have started to 'clear the way' towards improvements in operational performance. We have defined disruption properties – events, costs and their tangible and intangible causes. In this chapter, we will explain how this information should be organised to create tools for disruption monitoring, control and decision making, taking into account their quantitative and qualitative aspects. We will first look at the status of current information systems, explain why they cannot fulfil management needs for more comprehensive information about operational changes, and describe the basic requirements for system information and its main components. Problems associated with data accuracy will be tackled next, followed by a description of the intangible aspects of disruption information management. Finally, the chapter concludes with a summary of the benefits that the concept of disruption loss management can bring to airlines. By building the *system* knowledge about the volume and causes of deviation from planned operations, airline executives will get a better insight into its weaknesses, and will be able to monitor the results, prioritise decision, and coordinate improvement actions.

Many airlines resist the idea that controlling delays and disruptions is possible, due to the high level of uncertainty involved in airline operations. The truth is, however, that much of this 'uncertainty' is self-imposed, usually as a result of increased complexities and strategies that are not properly adjusted to airline operational capabilities. We have seen through practice that the operational environment becomes less uncertain for airlines with simplified operations and those who know how to minimise or avoid the negative effects of internal and external constraints. Our goal is to organise the disruption information in such a way that it can support airline efforts to minimise system weaknesses and reduce a self-induced uncertainties.

The more complex business and operational structures are, the more difficult they are to control. Airlines may invest in the best operational researchers, hire the best consultants, and have the best optimisation tools available today to help them improve operational performance, but this would not be enough to take them to the top of punctuality league tables or minimise disruption costs. It is obvious that many other aspects need to be taken into account to achieve better operational efficiency.

Among them is a good cross-functional relationship. Airlines that managed to soften departmental boundaries and vertical barriers in communication are able to more easily spot the problems, to learn from them and to make their recurrence less probable. Complex organisations have difficulties in establishing such relationships. In combination with the lack of integrated information and links between operational and strategic functions, senior executives face difficulties in understanding the real reasons behind operational problems and the way they change planned cost and revenue. In these circumstances, the executives' decisions could make current and future disruption situations even worse. For people involved in operations, it may seem that senior managers ignore their daily efforts to make flights operate on time, especially when despite their attempts to improve things, the total number of disruptions keep surging. This demoralises operations staff and alienates them from senior management.

Take the case of an airline where the ground operations managers and staff put a lot of effort into improving the poor on-time performance at one of its base airports. These local efforts did not improve punctuality, and in fact, the results were even worse. The majority of problems were caused by the supplier who was permanently short of staff and had inadequate ground equipment. The problem could not be resolved at station level and the message from ground operations managers did not get through to the senior executives, who were expected to provide some 'material evidence' about damages caused by the supplier. The problem at this base airport continued to disrupt not only flights operating to that airport, but also other parts of the network. It was only after a couple of ground incidents including costly aircraft damage that management became involved in resolving the problem. In the meantime, the airline incurred significant losses and damaged its market position resulting in a drop in revenue. Involving the senior decision makers at earlier stage obviously required more comprehensive information about the magnitude of problems in 'system' terms, and also reliable cost information to translate operational issues into a 'business case' and help resolve the issues more promptly.

This is only one of a myriad of cases where bringing the integrated information about system disruptiveness at functional levels before the eyes of senior executives could help resolve the system issues. Current information systems could hardly solve these problems, as their predominant objective is to satisfy requirements at functional levels. Let us take a closer look at issues related to current solutions and how they can be overcome.

## Current Solutions

Existing information systems are organised in a way that provides only a part of the answer to the disruption problem. Current applications, which contain most of the elements of operational irregularities like scheduling, operations control, maintenance, departure control, and crew planning, are not organised to provide information links with disruption properties necessary for their management and control. They are designed to satisfy specific operational functions, using flight schedule as their common denominator. For each of these applications, including optimisation processes, improvements are planned at functional levels, where even the best solutions do not guarantee the best system results.

Integration of basic operational software applications has always been on vendors' agenda despite airlines' scepticism. A senior operations executive at a Big Three US carrier said that the 'dream of completely integrated system that provides intelligent real time decision-making in SOC,[1] maintenance and airport operations is just that – a dream. There is a notion that at some point in the future this has to converge in an integrated system but it's just not out there. The decisions we make today are far more complex than the systems are integrated to handle' (Flint, 2001).

Airlines and vendors have put in lots of effort to optimise the process of schedule recovery, but not many of their solutions have proved to be reliable and used in practice to their true potential. Some of the most costly airline disruptions have been caused by implementation of optimisation tools, causing long cascading effects including months of reduced operations. Airlines can make improvements in operational efficiency as long as they invest in workable solutions, rather than wasting their time and money developing the impossible. Sabre's Chief Scientist Barry Smith said:

> The issue in operations is that you have a pretty complicated set of flows for aircrew, passengers and aircraft. There are an awful lot of possible solutions or recovery strategies for each component. If you are looking for a typical US domestic hub with complexes of 40 flights out, you're talking literally billions of possible solutions out there. Not surprisingly, identifying the best solution, whether in terms of recovery costs or passenger service impact, is just impossible. Even airlines with the best data processing systems tend to look at some relatively simple localised solutions that may work for a particular hub at a particular point in time but that may have some downline impacts either for that particular hub later in the day or tomorrow or at other stations around the systems.

It seems that major improvements in the development of information systems at operations level are not in sight. The situation is pretty much the same at the other end: strategic and corporate managers are not fully aware about the effects their decisions have on operational performance. Their efforts to establish these links are sporadic, usually related to loss recovery from third parties. This random, manually gathered, information is not systematic, depends on individual knowledge and skills, and may not be reliable.

From these points of view, the situation may seem incurable. But, what if we look at the problem from a different perspective? What if, instead of just being immersed in a myriad of daily problems as they occur, we step above operational to a strategic plane where operational plans are conceived? We could be able to see a bigger picture about disruptions, how they come into existence, and identify

---

1   Station Operations Centre.

those with biggest impact on airline cost and quality of service. We will surely be much more selective about where our attention goes, which can give us more time to focus on problems that really matter. We will also be able to better understand internal relationship, recognise airline, airport and ATC limitations from a higher perspective, recover losses caused by third parties and much more. This new approach to an unexplored area of airline management will create opportunities for airline executives to act selectively in resolving problems, and will support the learning processes. Let us look at the key system requirements of the disruption knowledge system.

## What Disruption Information Do Airlines Need?

Management decisions are made with the good intention of benefitting the business. However, with little evidence to support these decisions, the results can be quite the opposite. The main objective of a disruption information system is to empower airline managers with knowledge about the cost of operational changes and their underlying causes and help them better understand the impact of their decisions on the wider system performance.

The task of establishing the relationships between strategic plans, operational decisions, and airline financial performance may look too complex, especially in big organisations, and may put off many managers from even trying to understand these connections. However, managing an airline effectively without this knowledge is not possible. Methods explored in this book are aimed at simplifying this process by creating a system that will enrich operational information with elements of cost and revenue, and enable airline executives to be constantly informed about the cost-critical issues and their origins. This solution will promote the introduction of *system* thinking in daily practices. At the same time, it will support improvement of individual processes that constitute building blocks upon which system performance is based. Once this solution is created and implemented, airline executives will be in a position to coordinate efforts of every component of the system to produce the best overall result.

The system should provide a set of flexible executive reports about operational disruptiveness, including changes in planned costs with reference to problem areas. Instead of looking at disconnected segments of information coming from different parts of the organisation and trying to understand their interconnectedness, airline executives will be in a position to access the integrated disruption information and get answers to a wide variety of questions of a strategic, financial, commercial, technical and operational nature. They will also be able to better understand intangible aspects of disruption problems like competence, process coordination, and other related issues. By enabling a share of information about operational disruptions, and stimulating communication across the airline, the system will support the decision-making processes at various functional levels including top management.

The information structure to which decision makers can refer when trying to resolve disruption problems of a cross-functional nature should consist of the reliable hard information complemented with a set of tools that will create links between measurable and intangible information about the causes of operational disruptions. Hard information should be the anchor, the common reference from where it is possible to build structures that will help managers find more objective answers to their questions. It has to be organised and presented in a simple way so that experiential knowledge and soft information could be more easily put into the right context.

We will be searching for explicit and tacit sources of information to create the solution which can stimulate the right questions that provoke further questions about the true causes of disruptions and their consequences on costs, punctuality and other system parameters. This would allow airline executives to identify emerging patterns, and to:

- Gain wider factual knowledge about disruptions, their underlying causes and business consequences.
- Identify the qualitative elements related to disruptions and map their links with measurable values.
- Create shared understanding of the disruption problems by establishing links between operational and strategic processes.
- Improve collaboration among people involved in various functions and processes across the airline.
- Create a higher level of competences in managing operational changes and improving planning processes.

A system for disruption loss management needs to provide a timely, fact-based insight into the changes in planned operations. Access to integrated disruption information will create new prospects for cost saving and minimise exposure to losses due to inadequate internal processes and external events. The system links between strategic and operational environments should improve management awareness about the structure and amount of costs involved in their decisions. The results are more likely to create a sustainable competitive advantage than those resulting in more imitable tactics.

Despite the fact that in a majority of cases, disruptions generate 'losses', it is impossible to make the distinction between the 'disruption costs' and 'disruption losses' in situation when there is no reference to costs associated with disrupted operations. They are often described as 'costs' because they are currently an integral part of airline operating costs and cannot be, monitored and managed separately. Disruption costs are sometimes described as 'insurance policies' against irregularities extrapolated from the past together with other costs, or can be included in airline contingency plans, again without special reference to disrupted operations. We will be using both terms until method for differentiation between disruption losses and the rest of the costs is made clearer. The system for managing this information will therefore be called the 'Disruption Loss Management' (DLM). The method for disruption loss management will provide insights into the dynamic nature of airline operations and help elevate many of the disruption-related issues from operational to the corporate level, in a fast, comprehensive, and reliable way. Apart from the 'Disruption Information System' (DIS) that would provide the hard information, the DLM should also consist of tools that will support the analysis of intangible causes of disruptions.

## Main Components of a Disruption Loss Management System

In order to respond better to yet unknown forces of change, airlines need an information structure designed to support flexibility and adaptiveness, as it has to take into consideration ambiguity, inconsistency, multiple perspectives, and the temporality of the existing information. It should also allow for exploration of previous experiences that should be saved in the system's memory, as well as comparison of various disruption scenarios that will help envisage and resolve future problems.

*Information requirements*

The primary role of a disruption information system is to show how much and why the actual operation deviates from plan, operationally and financially. The building blocks of the system will be the elements described earlier as disruption properties, which need to be organised and linked into the system to provide comprehensive and up-to-date information about various aspects of operational disruptiveness. In order to fulfil these objectives, such a system needs to satisfy several basic requirements:

- Enable integration of planned and actual operational information with delta costs.
- Link operational changes with their reasons and delta costs.
- Provide a flexible reporting system on disruption cost, revenue and passenger experience, with timely access to disruption information.
- Create a platform for comparison of simulated operational scenarios.
- Allow integration with enterprise data to improve the quality of executive information systems.

Such an information system will provide comprehensive disruption information to the decision makers, help strengthen the links between operational and strategic processes, and promote a new cost saving culture. Corporate managers, strategists, and operational decision makers will be able to better understand various aspects of disruption problems, their 'cost weight', as well as passenger inconveniences.

A disruption information system will enable access to previously unavailable information, that will support diverse management action, such as measurable cost savings and loss recovery, disruption risk analysis, monitoring of operational and cost changes of budget plans, dynamic strategies, evaluation of operational efficiency, integration of internal functions and processes, continuous learning, among others.

One of the additional but still important roles of the system would be its use as a benchmark for optimisation tools. It could be a valuable aid in comparing disruption-related decisions with the same results provided by the existing optimisation systems and would support the improvement of optimisation solutions.

Methods for disruption loss management could contribute towards achievement of operational excellence by allowing airlines to constantly monitor operational and cost efficiency and offering the best possible service to airline customers.

*Basic information structure*

The concept of disruption loss management, at its core, is based on information about change in planned schedule defined by disruption properties. As soon as an operational decision to change the reference schedule turns into an 'event', it starts to affect passenger services, cost, and revenue. Every event can be triggered by one or more reasons and could be a consequence of direct and indirect causes described in Chapters 2 and 3. Operational events are a backbone of the disruption information system and, in information terms, serve as a link between disruption causes and delta costs. These basic disruption elements need to be built into the disruption information system that will be the starting point for failure analyses and support of the decision-making processes across the airline organisation. This concept is shown in Figure 4.1.

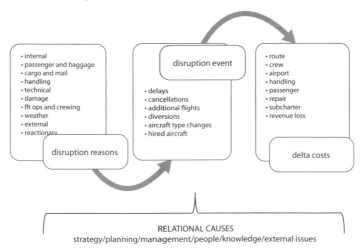

**Figure 4.1    Basic elements of disruption information system**

There are several issues that would need to be considered while structuring the basic system elements:

- The output will depend on choice of reference schedules: the closer it is to planned departure, the less disruptive will operations look. In general, there are two types of schedule changes that need to be taken into account: pre-planned schedule changes published in airline reservation and global distribution systems, and operational changes that occur closer to the departure time, and are usually not published. Both of these schedule changes create a part of the disruption information system, and are defined as operational events. However, it is important to make the distinction between the two for reporting and comparison purposes.
- One disrupted flight can be associated with several operational events, be it delays, diversions or aircraft type changes (see Table 4.1), but not every combination of operational events can be associated with each of the disrupted flights.
- Each event needs to be linked with one or more disruption causes and each disrupted flight should be classified as initial or reactionary, in order to mark the sequence in which they create a group of disruption events related to a single reason.
- Every reactionary flight must be linked with the preceding reactionary flight, and ultimately with the initial cause of disruption. These links can become more complex during the operations and may require formation of branches with several side levels of initial causes.
- Operational events have to be associated with the corresponding delta costs. As an example, a flight that was diverted, delayed, and had aircraft replaced with a different type due to a technical problem at the outstation, needs to be associated with change in crew cost, airport and handling charges, cost of aircraft repair by third party, passenger services, cost of positioning flights, fuel and ATC costs and revenue loss.

This structure is a base for the creation of a reporting system that needs to be flexible enough to satisfy various management needs. In order to improve the scope and quality of executive information, reports should be empowered by good

**Table 4.1     Operational event distribution**

| Flight No. | Operational event 1 | Operational event 2 | Operational event 3 |
| --- | --- | --- | --- |
| 11 | Delayed | Aircraft Type Changed | Diverted |
| 21 | Delayed | Subchartered | |
| 23 | Cancelled | | |

search and filtering functions, and enriched with information about commercial priorities and competition, event escapability, and level of data completion.

*Organising the data*

In order to satisfy management demand for comprehensive, reliable, and easy to use disruption information, it is crucial that the system includes all of the relevant data and information necessary to fulfil this demand. We have already explained that business complexity should not be an insurmountable obstacle, assuming that some compromises have to be made in order to eliminate less important issues that may clog the output. While most of the operational information can be collected using the automated systems, the airline-specific cost information may require more effort to be identified and collected from the source. The problem, however, may not be as complicated as it looks. It could be overcome in two ways, without significantly affecting the accuracy of output. Firstly, not all of the cost data affect the output in the same way. By applying the Pareto principle, the 'vital few' data should be separated from the 'trivial many'. Secondly, if the more accurate data take too long to gather and they do not significantly affect the accuracy of output, the system could initially be populated with the existing, or estimated cost data. Once the system is up and running, an airline can start to monitor the data relevance and their validity, and gradually improve the accuracy and content of information. The fact that a great deal of data is permanent or semi-permanent can ease off the problem. The most challenging part of the solution will be the automated integration of cost data. Some of the technology issues will be explained later in this chapter. But first, we need to understand how the disruption data could be identified.

*Identifying the data*   Deciding which data will be used by the system is an important step in creating the disruption loss management system. During this process, it would be necessary to:

- Identify disruption-related data.
- Define existing data stores – operational, scheduling, financial and local departmental applications and assess their quality and accuracy.
- Define data that is currently unavailable, like specific cost items or some reasons for disruption, and describe procedures for its collection.
- Specify data that requires manual input like causes of delays and actual departure times (when ACARS is not in use).
- Organise data gathering and establish discipline and control over its quality.

It is essential that airlines capture operational data as close to real time as possible. All data should be structured in a consistent way, allowing easy access and swift updates. The system should ensure easy data maintenance and updates, and should have the ability to quickly adapt to situations when changes in static and semi-static parameters associated with route structure, aircraft types and cost values become more frequent.

*Quality of data*   As we have seen earlier, much of the operational and cost data required for creation of the disruption information system is incomplete, out of date, or otherwise inadequate for answering critical business questions, and often do not deliver the right information to the right person at the right time. Consequently, planners, strategists and operational decision makers may drag the organisation into unknown losses without being aware about the consequences of their actions on important system parameters that are out of their scope.

But what defines the quality of data and information in the first place? We shall assume that the disruption data quality refers to the state of completeness, validity, consistency, timeliness, and accuracy. These elements of quality need to be well balanced in order to become useful. Accuracy on its own does not mean much if data is not delivered on time or is not complete. Balancing the elements of the quality of disruption data has always been a challenging task for airlines as it requires many skills and a good understanding of airline overall activities.

*Data gathering*   To create adaptable strategies and successfully manage disruptions, airlines rely on all kind of inputs. Some of these inputs are measurable, some are not easily accessible, and some cannot be quantified. Defining which data to collect, requires lots of balancing between its business values, level of accuracy, and amount of time needed to make them available to the decision makers. This process should be carefully planned and performed, as organisation of data capturing and control directly affect the reliability of output.

The time needed for its collection is dependent on availability of data, their quality, stage of automation and level of data integration, among many other factors. Elements that define level of data accessibility can be grouped in the three major categories. The first includes data that is directly accessible, like those contained in planned and actual schedules, standardised at industry level. They represent the foundation of a disruption information system. Secondly, there are local or industry databases with data such as fuel consumption, aircraft and airport data, number of booked and disrupted passengers, currency exchange rates and so on. Finally, the third level includes disruption costs and revenue data stored in various local applications. They are not generally standardised and are not captured at source (crew and passenger costs, fuel cost or revenue loss). Some of this data resides in legacy applications that could be directly integrated into the system, some may be stored in local spreadsheets, while some may not be captured at all.

Collecting the cost data is a demanding process, as it is dispersed throughout the organisation. However, not all of this data is of equal importance for the calculation of delta costs. Airlines need to decide which data is essential, how accurate it should be, and then build these criteria into the system for disruption loss control.

For airlines that do not favour information systems that take too long to implement, there should be a faster option with regard to data gathering. In order to 'quick-start' the system without perfecting each of the cost data, the system could initially be populated with values contained in the existing systems. If time allows, some of this data could be adjusted to the more accurate values. This approach would still be likely to bring benefits in comparison with previously non-existing disruption information. The mere fact that disruption costs will be linked with disruption events and with their root causes can contribute to improvements in managing disruptions and strengthen the cross-functional links. Data accuracy can then be improved gradually, at the airline's own pace.

*Data accuracy* The desired level of data accuracy should be a compromise between time and the cost associated with its processing. The problem mainly arises from the diversity of cost data that require more time to accurately allocate, integrate, update, and maintain. In order to be properly managed, disruption cost data needs to be well understood and its input knowingly simplified whenever its overall effectiveness is low. It should be measured by its impact on overall results against the time and costs involved in raising the level of accuracy. As an example, calculating accurately the increase in fuel costs generated by extended flight time while an aircraft is kept in a holding stack is quite a laborious process, as the locations at which fuel is purchased are frequently altered. It should require the introduction of additional procedures, system, and workload which may not justify the effort. If, say 20 per cent variance between the existing estimated values and accurate information about the actual fuel price would amount for only €50 per holding event[2] , the pursue for higher accuracy will not be justified, as saving generated by higher accuracy is smaller than additional investment in staff, tools, and time required for to achieve better accuracy.

Another example relates to the cost of crew accommodation. Capturing this cost accurately is a tedious task. Hotel rooms that are booked occasionally when disruptions occur would require manual input, while others contracted on annual or ad hoc bases may not be sufficiently utilised and could, in the end, come at higher cost. If, for example, the planned average cost of a single room amounts to €70, and its actual cost is €50, the variance for every 1,000 crew members would make it up to €20,000; the sum that is insignificant compared to the time and money involved in organisation of accurate data gathering and its contribution to overall results. It is much more important to associate estimated costs with disruption events and their initial reason.

It suggests that using the best cost estimates and adjusting them occasionally as close to reality as possible, could in some cases be the most reasonable solution. If a higher level of accuracy is ever required, airlines should be able to isolate cases that matter and manually improve the data accuracy. When using cost as

---

2   Estimate based on Eurocontrol figures on fuel and emission costs in Europe (Season 2004/05).

a measure of operational efficiency, and for disruption loss management, the 'accounting accuracy' is less important than understanding the key drivers behind the change in planned costs and their impact on airline financial results. Still, the accuracy of each of the disruption costs should pass the effectiveness test before it becomes a part of the system, and whenever possible, calculated with a high level of precision.

*Update dynamics*    In terms of dynamics, data could be categorised as permanent, semi-permanent and actual. Permanent data rarely changes, like basic information about aircraft and airports. Semi-permanent data needs to be updated annually or seasonally, and includes planned flight schedules and the majority of delta costs, like subcontracted services (airport and ATC charges, aircraft types and passenger handling charges), fuel prices, crew allowances, contracted hotel charges and so on. The third category of data changes more frequently, like hired aircraft, passenger compensations, and actual operational data.

The value of disruption information is dependent on two types of data input: automated and manual. While it is possible to acquire the majority of data automatically, the manual input can still have a great impact on accuracy of output. Some data, such as the reasons for disruptions are crucial for the reliability of delay reporting. The accuracy of the input will very much shape the quality of the output information about disruption causes and affect management decisions. In everyday life, the manual data input may be distorted from a variety of reasons, mainly due to a lack of information, and in some cases, opportunity to cover up for internal errors. Achieving the required level of accuracy of this data requires procedural guidance and random control. The US approach to reporting on causes of delays and cancellations sets an example of how this issue could be tackled. Faced with huge problems with inaccurate reporting on causes of airline delays, and under increased pressure to make this information public, the Department of Transportation required air carriers to file airline service quality performance reports under the regulations to collect and report the causes of airline delays and cancellations. The following instruction for data collection illustrates the level of details suggested to be included in airline reporting on causes of delay.[3]

> A flight was 30 minutes late pushing back from the gate. The 30-minute delay consisted of 10 minutes for a late arriving aircraft and 20 minutes for slow boarding process because of an oversales problem. The flight arrived 24 minutes late. The delayed flight would be coded 8 minutes for late arriving flight and 16 minutes for air carrier. Please note in this example that the 6 minutes gained after push back was prorated back to the two recorded delays. In this example, late arriving aircraft was 33.3 percent of the original delay and the air carrier delay was 66.6 percent of the delay. Therefore, late arriving aircraft was computed as

---

3    US Department of Transportation, 'Reporting the Causes of Airline Delays and Cancellations', *Federal Register*, 27 December 2001 (Volume 66, Number 248).

33.3 percent of 24 which equals 8; and air carrier was computed as 66.6 percent of 24 which equals 16.

This area deserves the special attention of airline managers. Much improvement can be made by specifying procedures for data input, setting organisational responsibilities, and introducing the practice of post-flight analysis with the support of 'scenario-builder', a tool that would allow simulation of various disruption scenarios and help with understanding the consequences of inadequate reporting on disruption causes on system performance.

*Data links*    Another important element of data input that affects the quality of system for disruption loss management is the link of reactionary with initial causes of disruptions. If this function is not well supported by the operations control application, and the company's procedures, it would leave lots of space for often unintentional improvisation during the recording phase and result in an extremely high number of unspecified reactionary changes in disruption reports. Reactionary delay code 93 which stands for 'aircraft rotation', or late arrival of aircraft from another flight or previous sector, appears to be the most popular among the recorded delay reasons and is a hiding place for many costly operational problems. The resulting inaccuracies could, for example, distort important information like the technical reliability of aircraft, which is usually coloured brighter than it actually is, and can seriously mislead the decision makers. In addition, a high percentage of unspecified reactionary reasons are a sure sign of poor operations management.

*Validation and system audit*    To ensure the effectiveness of a system for disruption loss management, airlines need to have a function for independent system audit. Internal audit should periodically review the validation process, including specific procedures, responsibilities, results, timeliness, and responsiveness to findings. It should be focusing on the depth, scope, and quality of the system for disruption loss management, review process and conduct appropriate testing to make sure that the conclusions of these reviews are well founded and report its findings at least annually to the senior executives.

*Data completeness*    While the system needs to deliver information that is as accurate as possible, some of cost data may take longer time to collect, especially those related to disrupted operation. The time required for these data to 'harden' will depend on the level of automation and agreed level of data accuracy. Insistence on a high level of data accuracy that has minor or no impact on the decision making could prevent managers from having access to any kind of cost information at the time they need it. The information system should be designed to avoid situations where management information is delivered too late just because, say, 5 per cent of low value data requires more time to be gathered. For example, the information about cost of passenger compensation claims typically required more time to be collected, but that should not stop the system from delivering timely reports about other readily available information. In order to maintain credibility of system output, however, users would need to be informed about the number of 'pending' events and, depending on the urgency, decide whether to wait for more accurate information or use the best estimates to make timely decisions. In any case, the level of accuracy needs to be traded-off against the cost of the time and value of getting the more precise information.

*Add-ons*   There is some optional information that, although not essential, can significantly enhance the value of output information and help with data filtering and the accuracy of the reporting system.

*Reporting flexibility*   Each of the output modules must be flexible enough to allow a variety of users to search through different system levels and within the different timeframes to get the information that can satisfy their individual needs.

*Filtering*   Among the main system objectives must be ability to separate unimportant information from things that matter most, according to preset criteria. It has been proven through practice that making decisions purely on statistical analysis, based on heaps of data and information or scientific documentation does not work well. The information needs to be filtered, easily accessible by people who need it. The system has to be flexible enough to allow answers to various questions that can arise during the decision-making process.

*Event escapability*   Marking a disruption event as avoidable makes it possible to separate events that require management attention, from those that are not possible to avoid. It is essential for airlines to make the distinction between avoidable and unavoidable losses generated by disruptions. Escapability needs to be determined at organisation level, as it requires understanding of wider system issues. Functional definitions may be too narrow to reflect the full scope of measures that need to be taken to resolve disruption problems. For example, operations controllers may define technical disruption as unavoidable. This is because there is not much they can do to avoid it. Strategic planners, however, may see the technical problem as an opportunity for improvement and will describe it as avoidable.

Disruption escapability should be approached from both ends, strategic and operational, with clearly defined distinctions. There are many avoidable causes that can be controlled from operational level, such as errors, omissions, and functional improvements. Carriers make all kinds of routine mistakes that cause disruptions: they send aircraft to already occupied stands, mess up the pushback sequence, take a two-hour delay in the morning, and then find that the crew is out of time just before the final departure in the evening. Schedule, network, and strategic planners, and senior, middle, and operational managers make their contributions to system imperfections – sometimes inescapable but sometimes avoidable. The list can go on and on, just indicating how much room there is for improvement.

Disruption escapability has to be evaluated in its entirety, disregarding the cross-functional boundaries, but will have little value if it is not a part of a comprehensive and reliable system for disruption loss management.

*Alerts*  The scarcity of management time and huge amount of row information does not always allow airline executives to closely monitor changes of operational and cost parameters that may require their attention. This problem could be overcome by setting the disruption cost alerts, which will draw the attention of senior managers whenever the consequences of disrupted operations cross the critical line.

*Route coding*  One of the factors that can enhance the value of the decision-making process in operations is assigning the priority codes to major routes that need to be protected during the process of schedule recovery. Each route should be categorised according to its relative strategic value and incorporated into the disruption loss information system. This information could be also useful for operational and strategic decision makers who would be better able to adjust their strategies after evaluating the effect of flight disruptions on individual routes.

*Main system functions*

The main system functions should be organised through several modules, covering the requirements for: event monitoring and control, executive and departmental reporting, disruption analysis, loss recovery from third parties, scenario builder,

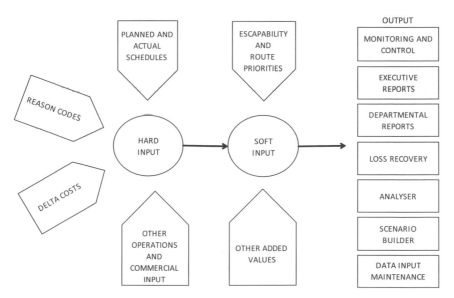

**Figure 4.2    Disruption information system – basic concept**

and modules for data input, maintenance, and administration (see Figure 4.2). Managers should be able to search through aggregate information, and be able to quickly access the filtered data to find the answers to their questions.

In order to satisfy diverse requirements for information across the company, the system should consist of the following five output modules:

*Disruption monitoring and control*   The system for disruption loss management should enable daily scanning of disrupted flights and associated events. It needs to display details about each disrupted flight, variable costs linked to specific operational events and promote the association of reactionary disruption events with their causes, allowing for quality control of data input, including the coding of disruption reasons. This is the place where ambiguous, incomplete, or unconnected data and information could be managed allowing for data monitoring, input of missing data, control of data links and 'soft' inputs. This module needs to be presented in a simple and user-friendly way, with a good filtering function

*Disruption reports*   Based on integration of planned, operational and cost data, the system ought to offer a set of flexible executive and departmental reports, to support the analysis of various aspects of disruptions.

*Executive reporting*   Airline executives must be able to continuously monitor changes in operational performance in order to identify problems at an early stage, rather than waiting to conduct periodic analysis of the business dictated by financial schedules. Executive reports should provide timely, high level information about overall results, pointing out to the causes of the most critical aspects of disrupted services. They would need to show how many passengers experienced long delays and cancellations, how much of the revenue was lost, and what are the most disrupted routes and airports. Executives should also be able to focus on avoidable cases, and monitor their monthly and seasonal trends. With an easy access to more detailed information, they will be in a position to understand how disruptions can cascade through the system, identify events, airports, and aircraft that triggered highest costs, and be able to more precisely evaluate risks of operational losses. By having a direct access to information and continuously monitoring changes in airline costs and causes, airline executives will be better equipped with knowledge about operational issues, ongoing system vulnerabilities, and take a more active role in disruption prevention.

The regular supply of information on changes in variable costs to corporate and resource planners is essential for dynamic adjustments of budget plans. Financial planners should be able to see their impact on every cost item, understand the reasons behind these losses, and make their plans less 'static'.

*Disruption analysis*   Analysis modules will provide the possibility for a wide range of analysis, from operational to strategic. The structure of this module should be adjusted to the various analytical requirements. It needs to be flexible, allow fast access to multilayered information and answer as many analyst's questions as possible. The following is a description of several possible analysis modules.

*Disruption cause analysis*   This module will provide analysts with answers to questions about the cost critical causes of disruptions in terms of losses and volume, and also the magnitude of their cascading effects on airline operations. It should be possible to see how many flights have been affected by each of the specified reasons, and how much money was lost. Like all other modules, it requires good sorting, filtering, and drill-down functions to provide the right answers to multi-layered questions related to disruption causes. This module will help reveal the full scale disruption causes have on other operational parameters and on passengers. It should be the starting point for the true root cause analysis.

*Operational event analysis*   An event module will enable a direct access to information about costs and revenue loss associated with delays, cancellations, hired aircraft, and other operational events. With ability to access this information, analysts will better understand the primary causes of delays, cancellations and other operational changes, their links with airport and aircraft limitations. It will also be possible to scrutinise the quality of decisions made during schedule recovery.

*Disruption analysis by sector*   This analysis module will offer access to various information about the volume of disruptions, number of affected passengers, cost and lost revenue at sector level. From here, analysts can enquire details related to the worst affected flights by volume of disruptions, costs, or revenue loss, uncover the effects of hub airports on route economics, discover operational bottlenecks, the effectiveness of block time policies, and much more. This information is vital for planning and decision making from various perspectives – strategic and network as well as marketing and operational.

*Disruption analysis by aircraft*   Information contained in this module should focus on disruption costs and causes associated with aircraft type, version, and each individual aircraft. It can reveal which aircraft were most often involved in initial disruptions, at which airport, why did it happen, how much it affected the airline costs, or may provide information about the effects of an aging fleet on airline operational and cost efficiency.

*Loss recovery*   The purpose of a loss recovery module is to fulfil airlines' specific need for information about direct and indirect losses caused by third parties through aircraft damages, late aircraft delivery, consequences of computer system failures, or ground equipment and staff shortages. They normally incur high indirect costs that should be compensated by, or more equally shared with, the third parties.

Among these causes, aircraft damage deserves special attention due to the volme of costs involved in damage incidents that include direct costs related to aircraft repair and, often more costly, indirect damages related to losses incurred by operational changes while damaged aircraft was out of service. The resulting report should be used to document losses that should be claimed from insurance companies, or from the third parties. The technique applied in these cases requires that operational recoveries related to damage incidents are frozen as soon as necessary adjustments related to these particular events are made, to avoid interference with other operational changes.

*Scenario builder*    During the planning process, airlines make number of predictions based on results achieved during previous year. This annual feedback, however, has limited relevance for resolving the issues related to the disruptiveness of airline operations. Traditional reports help planners and decision makers to learn from the past, but they are based on a repeated set of circumstances, rather than unfamiliar situations that airlines may face every day. These practices look backwards to a period that is too long to be relevant as a reference for planning in fast-changing operational environment, and needs to be complemented with a forward-looking orientation where managers will learn to 'see' future changes by creating scenarios with a variety of external and internal situations and inputs. Variations in scenarios can open executives' minds to the range of possible situations that may happen, and make them better prepared to cope with, and adjust to new circumstances.

The planning process needs to be more dynamic, and airlines should constantly be identifying problems and developing responses by building the scenarios. As an integral part of a disruption information system, scenario builder should support the decision-making processes, covering a wide range of operational scenarios. By sharing the same database with the disruption information system (planned and actual schedule, aircraft and airport database, variable costs and other operational parameters), it would create a universal platform for decision-making processes, linking operational solutions with business performance.

Scenario builder would open the possibility for the creation of a wide range of scenarios based on changes in operational parameters, and could be used for comparative analyses as diverse as:

- Hub efficiency;
- Comparisons of cost efficiency of aircraft and air routes;
- Cost effectiveness of changes in route plans;
- Effects of change in fuel prices;
- Operational decision making;
- Post-flight analysis;
- Contingency planning.

In addition, with the support of scenario builder it would be possible to isolate operational changes made during the disruptions caused by third parties and use them as evidence for compensation claims, together with calculation of indirect losses incurred during disrupted operations.

Scenario builder would be especially useful to support the continuous learning process by simulating real time events from the past that can be projected into the future with changed circumstances, so that airline managers can better understand the impact that operational changes have on business performance and passengers. It could be also used for training of personnel involved in operational decision making, who would be able to compare the results of various operational solutions and learn about their impact on airline costs and passengers.

*Data input, maintenance, and administration* This module should enable monitoring and maintenance of the static data and data sources, as well as other administrative functions. It should also facilitate integration with a wide range of data sources.

## Technology and Data Integration

In this section, we will look at the way in which disruption information can be organised and integrated into a single computerised system. We will introduce a new direction in which solutions for disruption management should be developed with special attention to data integration.

The system for disruption loss management will essentially bring together data from various sources within the organisation in order to allow detailed information on costs and causes of airline operational disruptions to be gathered, and in turn enabling decision makers to view and analyse it. Access to this information will be through standard and flexible reporting at departmental and corporate level and decision support modules. It would allow planners to evaluate the impact of their decisions, and assist operations personnel with real-time operational decisions (responding to disruptions, for instance). Thus, an assessment of the feasibility of implementing a disruption loss management system must include: choice of platform for the application used to gather the DLM system-specific data, information integration framework, reporting framework and business intelligence tools.

*Ease of integration with data sources*

One of the most important aspects of deploying the disruption loss management system will involve links with airline data sources. This process needs to be facilitated in a number of ways:

- Support for a wide variety of data storage systems – data source integration mechanisms have matured as technologies, providing support for a full range of database management systems.
- Data sharing – some of data used by DLM is not proprietary to individual airlines (airport and some route information or various distribution systems

for instance). There is thus scope for up-to-date data to be supplied to customers as a service using web-based distributed software technologies, or for sourcing the data from industry-standard providers. This would significantly simplify the integration process, and minimise the resources needed at the client's end to deploy and maintain the product.

• Integration with other solutions like operations control applications.

## Platform

The disruption loss management solution would be useful at all levels and sections of the organisation, and as such, it makes sense to enable the full range of users to quickly and easily gain access to it. It should be developed as a web application, accessed through the web browser and deployed on the airline's own web server – a centralised location-based architecture that will also make integration with data sources easier. A full range of reports would be accessible to anyone on the company's intranet with appropriate access privileges. Centralised architecture will dramatically simplify the software update and management process. The remote deployment of new releases, updates or patches will eliminate the need for on-site installation and customer-specific customisation, and incurs minimal maintenance costs. The system will allow a rapid and efficient implementation tailored to individual airline needs. Among other requirements, minimal time and resources will be required to get the application up and running. It will promote information sharing and re-use and could be integrated with airline enterprise data

The data and flexible reports produced by the disruption loss management system should be available in a variety of formats, and integration with a range of local applications should be supported by business intelligence tools. In addition, an API (Application Programmers' Interface) enabling developers to access key functionality needs to be made available. This will allow the disruption loss management system to be used as an input to other applications and models.

## Integration with other systems

The system for disruption loss management could be fed with data from scheduling, operations control, crew, and flight planning systems. It should be able to automatically import full-schedule files SSIM (Standard Schedules Information Manual), an industry-standard source of up-to-date schedule information. In addition, the integration work of the disruption loss management concept and the operations control application would provide a comprehensive source of actual operational data. Taken together, automated access to scheduling and operational information via SSIM files and operations control applications would create a powerful base for disruption analysis and management, enabling the software to automatically identify operational disruptions and assign appropriate default costs.

It will then enrich the operation control application with cost values enabling much more reliable decision support.

By allowing for human control in all phases of disruption data and decision management, it will gradually build a more robust system, simultaneously supporting development of more sophisticated optimisation tools. The integrated information will bring new values into the decision-making processes, not only at operational, but also at network, scheduling, strategic and finance levels. The disruption loss management and operations control integrated solution will provide increased value of the existing disruption recovery and management decision support solutions, such as:

- Benchmark for evaluation of operations control optimisation tools.
- Supplement to optimisation tools that will enable viewing of effects of optimisation results.
- Significant decrease in cost of software maintenance.

### How will DLM work?

We have looked so far at the elements of the disruption management system, and will now explain how these components need to be put together to make the system work.

Relevant corporate data and the disruption system application need to be organised into a single information system. The system for disruption loss management then gathers up-to-date data covering numerous factors affecting variable cost for each operational change and event. The resulting information on changes in variable costs and causes of disruptions would become instantly available for monitoring, quick reporting, comprehensive analysis, and various ad hoc queries. In addition, the disruption loss management system should allow decision makers to leverage the information stored within its database to create disruption scenarios – effectively mock-ups of real-life or expected disruption events that facilitate planning, cost estimation and risk management.

Disruption data may be gathered through an automated process or entered manually. The choice will depend on the availability of relevant information, technical feasibility, and the amount of disruption data typically generated. Similarly, static data used by the system – airports, aircraft, routes, costs, and so on – can be maintained manually or sourced from another system where possible.

The entire model for disruption loss management will rely on data from the following departmental systems:

- Network/fleet/schedule planning;
- Operations planning and control;
- Finance, strategic and corporate planning;
- Reservation systems;
- Engineering;

•   Customer relations.

Although the model for disruption loss management would be able to utilise all the sources of data listed above, it is important to note that an organisation can benefit from the model even without the full set of specified data sources. This may be required if an organisation has no interest in tracking every aspect of operational costs, or if certain information cannot be gathered or accessed electronically.

A system for disruption loss management does require a minimum set of information in order to give meaningful results. This consists of:

•   Planned and actual operational details (operational parameters and traffic volumes).
•   A subset of budgeted and actual costs and revenue.

This information could come from the existing systems where possible, being either periodically imported into DLM, or through real-time data integration. A disruption loss management system can additionally provide facilities for a subset of this data to be entered manually.

Disruption properties are dependent on operational parameters contained in airline schedule and operations applications (aircraft, airports, sectors). This data will be contained in an operational data store, permanent data store and semi-permanent data store.

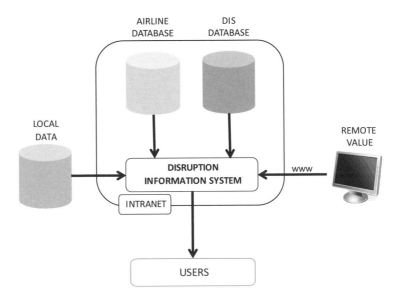

**Figure 4.3    Disruption information system scheme**

The system should facilitate the integration of a wide variety of airline data across the full range of data storage technologies, providing more detailed information about disruption problems. (system scheme is shown in Figure 4.3)

*Distribution*

One of the key features of a system for disruption loss management would be its ability to send the right reports to the right people at the right time. Using the current technology, companies can manage and control personalised distribution of all forms of business information to a broad community of recipients.

This system will help decision makers to learn more about operational dynamics, the way disruption problems were resolved and how this information could be used to minimise future losses. However, one should remember that this model is only a tool among other tools that should be used to help communicate the process of decision making and stimulate learning. Airlines will still face a considerable challenge in gathering disruption data and should make sure that it is regularly scrutinised. For this reason, the best approach for airlines that are only beginning to use this strategy is simply to start somewhere, even if that means adopting a simple approach.

## How Much to Invest in Data Accuracy?

How much should airlines invest in data accuracy? Current airline information systems are not built nor organised and integrated to support the function of disruption management at higher organisational levels. The scope and accuracy of disruption-related information provided by costly optimisation tools is difficult to evaluate, often excludes important factors outside the operational environment, and is therefore rarely trusted by the decision makers. On the other side, the manually gathered information about the most costly disruptions is based on too many assumptions, is incomplete, time consuming, highly dependent on individual knowledge and skills, and therefore not sufficiently reliable in system terms. The data accuracy is valued differently by different airlines. The more knowledgeable and less complex the organisation, the better real values of disruption information are understood and more cautious the management is in acquiring unrealistic solutions to disruption problems. And not every airline is in a position to invest a vast amount of money in costly tools to get the more accurate information. After all, even the most expensive of these tools and high level of technical expertise may not to be enough to produce the highest levels of output accuracy.

The core of the problem could be in the way the solution to information problem is approached. It is often associated with management and vendor desires to get the *big* solutions, *big* projects with *big* expectations squeezed into a very little timeframe – mix all this together, add insufficient time to get the data right, do not involve the right people in the project, and there is a recipe for failure. Developed by external specialists generically, these solutions can rarely satisfy an airline's diverse needs. As a result, subjectivity in decision making prevails over knowledge and is often dictated from the position of power. This can answer the question why it takes so long to make system improvements and why so many 'big projects' aimed at decreasing the number of flight delays, or making effective cost cutting, rarely materialise.

The question is what can make airline decisions more effective and in line with their core objectives? Instead of thinking 'big' when it comes to solutions for multi-dimensional problems, airlines need to adopt the stepped approach strategies. Development and implementation of complex solutions need to be done in stages. Smaller workable parts with measurable results have much bigger value than systems that promise much and do little for the airline. The comparison of several steps that lead to improvements in data accuracy and their effects on the investments is shown in Figure 4.4. It suggests that on the way to improving data accuracy the airline can do better by balancing between investments and accuracy, rather than making large investments and still not reaching 'total' accuracy.

We have so far explained what disruptions are, their properties and how to organise hard data into a management system that will provide a 'multi-dimensional' and timely access to disruption information. Instead of overloading managers with information, the system will provide the timely and targeted output. This 'hard' information, however, needs to be complemented with intangible information about indirect causes of disruptions, which will be described in the following section.

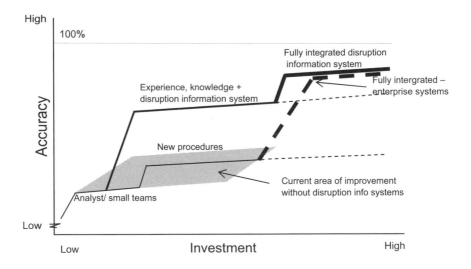

**Figure 4.4    Investment in accuracy**

**Mapping the Process**

Current information systems provide the basis for describing problems that have occurred, but not the explanation. Managers know what the deviations of budget plan are, but they may not know how to minimise them. They are informed about the increase in crew costs, but not what drove them. Moreover, the emphasis on the hard information tends to discourage the consideration of a whole range of factors described as indirect causes of disruptions which are softer, but could be more critical for strategy and decision making. The point is that much of the information important for strategists cannot be turned into figures. The lack of knowledge, experience, poor staff morale, or insufficient training, may be information that departmental managers are aware of, but how these weaknesses affect the system often remains unknown. This is why managers at higher organisational levels spend a great deal of time developing their own personal information system, building the networks of contacts and information of all kinds. The question is, what kind of personal information system about disruptions can they build when neither much of the hard, nor soft, information about disruptions is available?

Obviously, there is no shortage of information about disruptions. The problem is how to extract the right information and even more importantly, how to interpret it. Imagine yourself sitting in the pilot's seat of an Airbus 340. All the flight information is there to help you fly, but you still cannot get the plane in the air. Without knowing how to use that information, knowledge is not power.

Getting the hard information is often not enough to resolve complex issues. Executives need some sort of useful guidance for solving unstructured problems. In order to resolve them, decision makers will need to complement computable information with less tangible data. Answers to questions about high costs of disruptions caused by operational reasons normally lead to more questions about underlying causes of problems, planning and operational constraints, which the disruption loss management *system*, not just a disruption information *tool*, needs to provide. Mapping the links between operational causes, losses and intangible causes hidden within departmental functions, processes, and people will let decision makers 'see' and better understand these links. This will surely influence the quality of intuitive decisions, which we all constantly make.

There are many different techniques that can be used to describe the relationship between disruption losses and their drivers hidden behind various departments, processes, and other non-coded reasons. They can help even inexperienced persons to quickly grasp the interconnection of disruption-related processes and improve the quality of decision-making.

It is important to understand that there are no 'one-fit-all', static relationship maps. They are airline specific, and change in line with internal and external circumstances, organisation, and people. Once established, they will become a valuable guide for decision making. They will also preserve previous experiences and practices – the reference points from which progress can be measured.

They will promote the system knowledge about internal dependencies, but also knowledge that will inspire new ideas about preventing or reducing operational risks that lead to disruptions.

The map in Figure 4.5 shows the links between operational reasons of disruptions and locations within organisations that may have caused them in the first place. It shows that, for instance, origins of disruptions caused by crew shortage should be traced further than just in operations departments. At a deeper level, sources of problems could be the result of strategic trade-offs incorporated into network and schedule plans, inadequate organisation and procedures, underinvestment in crew, problems with support information tools, lack of internal communication, or introduction of new work time regulations that the airline has not properly

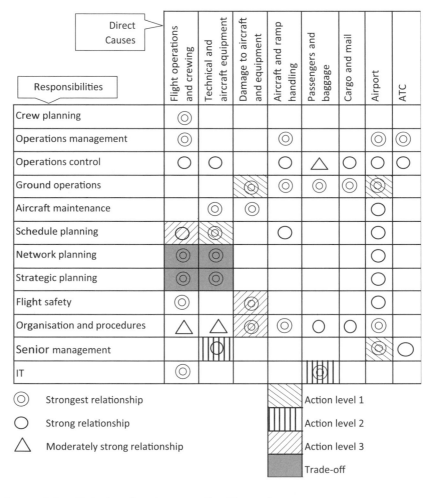

**Figure 4.5    Relational action map for disruption management**

implemented. All of these situations could happen simultaneously. The action to alleviate their negative effects can only be taken if they are recognised as problems. The 'healing' process should also take care of other parts of the system and, indeed, of the whole airline. It requires good coordination at the top level of the organisation from where it is possible to see the bigger picture.

In order to avoid subjectivity in prioritising actions, they should be initiated according to the magnitude of damage they cause to system performance. They may include the volume of losses over a certain period of time, high number of delays and cancellations on certain routes, problems originating at certain airports or aircraft, cost of passenger complaints and compensations, and so on.

DLM reports and maps are important tools in promoting dialogue among the board, senior management, and departmental managers. They should be reviewed frequently by the top-management team and periodically by the board to help them decide whether the current level of disruption costs can be tolerated.


## How to Benefit From a Disruption Loss Management System?

It would be an illusion to think that disruption problems could ever be completely resolved. What can be done, however, is to put a system in place that enables access to information that matters most, and achieve the level of accuracy that represents optimal balance between its value, time and the costs needed to acquire it.

The system for disruption loss management will help airline managers to recognise tangible and intangible risks of loss events, identify the problems beneath the surface, to look in more detail at what is going on operationally and financially, and control negative influences. It is not just an operational information system that brings disruption information before the eyes of managers for decision-making; it is the information and knowledge network that spreads through an organisation that is required to decode problems shown in operational output.

Airlines spend too little time defining the business side of disruption problems, and too much time coming up with operational solutions that rarely solve the problems. With the right amount of hard data and equipped with experiential knowledge, executives will be able to learn how to be selective with information and eliminate everything that is unimportant. The disruption loss management system will reveal the root cause of disruption problems and their subsequent effects. It will provide a structured approach, ensuring that no important cause is overlooked. It will also focus on identifying contributing factors to the problem, assuring that all significant causes are identified and will be an aid in preventing recurrence of problems.

While the importance of models and data in quantifying disruptions may be quite apparent, the importance of the intangible aspects may be less so. These aspects, however, are no less important for efficient operation. Factors like experience and judgement, affect what one does with model results. It is important that we understand that models cannot make the decisions, they are just tools, because in many cases it is the combination of management experience and models that helps to limit losses.

Emergent disruptions sometimes defy both hard data and intuition. People usually have no shortage of explanations for such surprising behaviour ('Of course we have so many delays when airport and ATC capacities are restricted!'). The crucial point here is that if we want to make real improvements in airline operational performance and minimise the risk of high disruption losses, we must start with a credible source of hard information. It can help us be more objective while examining the true causes of disruption problems. Airlines should, for example, become more aware about their contribution to the airports and airspace congestion, and incorporate this knowledge into their future plans.

The introduction of a system for disruption loss management should help carriers recognise variations that can hinder improvements in operational performance and eliminate wasteful activities. It will provide the glue to hold the information values hidden in various systems across the organisations, and stick the important pieces of information missing from the existing systems together.

By building the system that will provide airline executives with knowledge about disruptions, their real causes, and consequences on planned resources and ultimately costs, airlines will be able to renew their plans so that avoidable blocks are removed and operations run more smoothly. This process must be continuous due to volatility of the operational environment. It requires systematic action in preserving the diverse knowledge and experience of situations that can reoccur, by creating a system through which individual knowledge and experience could be integrated and accessible to the decision makers at various organisational levels.

Among many benefits the system for disruption loss management can bring to an airline, let us mention just a few: introduction of new cost-saving opportunities, raising awareness among airline management and staff of the structure and amount of costs involved in their decisions, facilitate process integration and communication, and support activities on introduction of industry standards for disruption control.

# Chapter 5
# Streamlining Disruptions

'There are 13 different industries within air transport. All of them make money apart from airlines ... Making money in this industry is not going to be that easy. We have to reduce our costs by between 20–30 per cent' said Professor Newal Taneja in his speech during one of the IATA meetings in 2002, a statement that is still fully valid. Streamlining disruptions is a step in that direction.

Aviation is one of the most advanced industries in technical terms. Its organisation and functioning is fascinating – advanced technologies driven by highly trained and licensed professionals, pilots, engineers, and air traffic controllers, with work procedures, performance audits and discipline developed to a level unprecedented in the business world. Every day airlines are safely transporting millions of passengers worldwide. Yet, they fail to deliver on the ordinary: over half of flights do not depart or arrive as originally planned – not an impressive score for such an industry.

The years' long decline in the quality of operational performance is a big cause for concern – it does not only affect flight punctuality, but has a significant effect on airline costs. Shedding light on this grey area of airline management may support airline efforts to reduce operating costs and improve flight punctuality and regularity.

We have seen so far how the information about changes in airline operations, their root causes and delta costs, could be brought to the attention of senior executives. Comprehensive information about disruptions embodied in DLM can help executives to understand how and why scheduled operations change, and how much it affects planned costs – much before the official company's figures are published and thoroughly analysed from the top. This can make it possible to address problems and their underlying causes in a timely manner, assign responsibilities, and follow the progress of actions taken to alleviate them.

In this chapter, we will describe the ways airline operations can be made less disrupted and more cost efficient. We will examine how much the simplification and focus on important issues can help airlines to streamline their operations, will explain how to use a disruption information system to measure airline operational efficiency, and look at some management and organisational issues that are prerequisite for successful implementation of disruption management.

There are three principles that have proved to work well in many organisations and that score high on the list of most successful companies. They are:

*   **Simplification** of business processes, where best results come from simplified but not simplistic systems.

- **Focus** on changes that have greatest impact.
- **Measure wide** and compare things that matter most.

Let us explore how each of these principles works for airlines.

### Simplifying the Process

There is a natural tendency for business to become too complex. All big organisations, especially large legacy airlines are inherently inefficient. Preoccupied with solving the complex problems, their attention is often drifted away from very basic things, like adding value to their customers.

Complexity increases the number of trivial activities, making it difficult for senior managers to recognise and focus on things that deserve their attention. They can get easily involved in ad hoc operational problems that could be resolved at local level, instead of spending their valuable time more effectively by making a small number of powerful interventions that can have a massive positive impact on the volume of operational disruptions. By following this principle, every organisation will realise great potential for cost saving and be able to offer better value to customers, both in price and in punctuality.

There is a big obstacle to this – many managers enjoy and thrive on complexity. Richard Koch put it this way: 'Most organisations, even ostensibly commercial and capitalist ones, are conspiracies of management against the interest of customers, investors, and the outside world generally. Unless firms are facing an economic crisis, or have an unusual leader who favours investors and customers rather than his or her own managers, excess management activity is virtually guaranteed' (Koch 2006, 101). The chances of increasing complexity are much greater in airlines with a diversified fleet and network, and with lack of integrated information. A good way to understand the effects of business complexity on airline operational and financial performance is by comparing the operational and cost efficiency of legacy and low-cost airlines.

Airline operating models have a direct impact on punctuality, currently the only measure of airline operational efficiency. In purely operational terms, there are two extreme models characterised by hub networks operated predominantly between primary airports by mixed fleet of traditional airlines, and point-to-point networks flown between secondary and tertiary airports by single aircraft type, typical for the true low-cost carriers. The space in between is filled by numerous airlines operating hybrid models. The comparison of punctuality and profit margins of airlines representing three different operating models (Ryanair, easyJet and British Airways) shown in Figure 5.1, where easyJet is categorised as a hybrid airline, demonstrates that the differences in punctuality and profit margins works in favour of simpler business models. We will further explore the wider aspects of traditional and low-cost operating models, their impact on airline performance, and

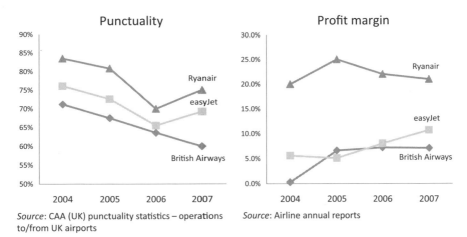

**Figure 5.1    Punctuality vs profitability, comparison of airlines with different operating models**

look at the way one of traditional carriers improved its punctuality and operational efficiency by carrying out a major network restructuring.

The true low-cost carriers have introduced simplification into the airline industry. By operating simple, point-to-point networks from less congested airports with simple fleet structures, flat organisations and cost effective ways of selling their product, they made big savings in operating costs, which allowed them to significantly cut prices, stimulate air travel, and penetrate deep into the market of traditional network airlines. They have radically changed the ways of running an airline. Many traditional functions ceased to exist, and planning and operational processes have become simpler, with less management levels and functional separation. Low-cost principles eliminated the need for complex network analysis, and have reduced the problems associated with flight connectivity, operational flexibility of multiple aircraft types and related crew and maintenance problems. These strategies have automatically reduced the possibility to make errors and omissions characterised by decision making in complex systems. On the other hand, managing airlines that operate these models is faced by challenges to keep the basic elements of simplicity during the fast expansion strategies, and constantly motivate already highly productive staff to do more. The complexities resulting from continuous expansion at rates above average have inevitably affected, to a more or less degree, the operational efficiency of low cost carriers. Still, their operational efficiency is high enough to outperform the results of traditional airlines.

According to Booz Allen and Hamilton, low-cost carriers spend 7 to 8 cents per seat mile for a 500–600 mile trip – half the cost of the average carriers operating a hub-and-spoke network for the same flight. About 70 per cent of this cost difference is attributed to the explicit choice of business model; it does not come just from employing lower paid staff or flying to less costly airports. Simplicity of fleet structure and network model drives many other costs down, including the number of employees, crew and maintenance costs, ground handling, and sales-related costs. An important contributor to the decrease in operating cost is the less disrupted operation, which is a valuable indicator of airlines' operational and cost efficiencies.

Over the years, legacy airlines have been adding layers of products and processes that despite aggregate revenue increases often could not outweigh the additional costs. Their network and fleet structures are traditionally designed to attract a high volume of connecting passengers, causing massive concentration of traffic at hub airports and inefficient utilisation of people, airline, airport, and airspace capacities. However, the fierce competition of low-cost carriers has forced many of them to start transforming their strategies. The ideas are diverse, from removing scheduling constraints (introducing the rolling hubs and longer, more random connections), network simplification (converting the existing connecting traffic to more direct routes), less diverse fleet structures, introduction of product differentiation between high and low priced services, to consolidations and mergers. The question is, how far could well-established legacy airlines go with strategic transformations by applying the principles of network and fleet simplification, and would the effort be justified by improvements in quality of service, and operational and financial result? One of the examples is the transformation carried out by Delta Air Lines in 2005, known as 'Operation Clockwork',[1] the largest network and operational redesign in aviation history. It sheds useful light on the effects projects of this type can have on improvement in airline operational efficiency.

Following serious financial and operational difficulties in an increasingly competitive market, Delta Air Lines decided to simplify its business model to compete better with the fast growing low-cost competitors. In 2004, overall operational performance reached low levels mainly due to limitations of airport, airspace, and runway capacities at their home base – the largest airline hub in the world – Atlanta Hartsfield-Jackson. The airline's objectives to grow profitably without additional capital expense and improve schedule reliability, was achieved by implementation of a new network and schedule structure. A total of 59 per cent of the network was rescheduled. The 'continuous hub' schedule combined with a reduced turn time operation significantly improved aircraft and facility utilisation. The scheduling efficiencies drove a 10 per cent increase in daily aircraft utilisation, freeing up 19 aircraft to be reinvested back into the network for additional revenue generation opportunities. The benefit of those 19 aircraft was in the range of $500 million dollars in capital that did not need to be invested. Additionally, eight gates and parking positions that did not exist under the current network design were freed up, allowing the capacity to grow with the 19 aircraft. By eliminating the scheduling peaks and smoothing the capacity throughout the day, the hub absorbed

---

1    Petraccione, L. (2007) *Delta Operation Clockwork* (Transportation & Logistics Practice, Decision Strategies, Inc).

over 80 additional departures per day (with a potential for over 40 more) without adding any resources (headcount or equipment). Maximising the use of all assets provided the capability for future growth of over 120 daily flights. Productivity improvements yielded staffing models with less idle time and overall greater asset utilisation of facilities, people and aircraft. Excluding fuel, the direct operating cost per available seat mile (DOCASM) decreased with the higher productivity of all assets. Revenue increased as compared to the previous banked structure. By 2007, the transformation resulted in hundreds of million dollars in both revenue and cost improvements for the company. As a result of this change, the system operational performance and reliability averaged 10 points higher for arriving aircraft and 15 points higher for departing aircraft when the continuous schedule model was first introduced (based on zero departure reference). The comparison of punctuality results of major US carriers shown in Figure 3.1 illustrates Delta's dominant position over its 'legacy' competitors.

Another example illustrates the effect of a simplified operating model on punctuality. It is based on a comparison – of a traditional airline with base at a congested hub (British Airways), and a point-to-point carrier based at the less congested Luton airport (Silverjet), both operating the same route between London and Newark, New Jersey. The results refer to a short period of three months, when it was possible to collect the data and use this rare opportunity to compare the effectiveness of airlines with such diverse business models, operating between the same city pairs. The difference is obvious (see Figure 5.2), and clearly illustrates the effects of simplified models on airline operational performance. These results should not be undermined by the fact that Silverjet ceased to exist in the middle of 2008 under the pressure of the rampant increase in fuel prices and fierce competition, which, as a young low-cost airline, Silverjet could not survive. By looking at the annual punctuality results on this route, only 53.62 per cent of all flights departed on-time (within 15 minutes) in 2007, a sharp decline from 73.8 per cent achieved in 2003 (UK CAA statistics).

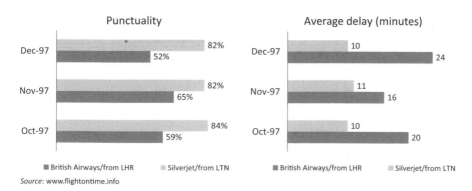

*Source*: www.flightontime.info

**Figure 5.2    Comparison of punctuality and length of delay for long-haul, traditional and low cost operators on London–Newark route**

Many airlines described as low-cost operators do not follow the essential low-cost principles. With a constant tendency to expand, low-cost carriers are stretching their business model by broadening their original market focus. They may add additional aircraft type, create some sort of connecting traffic, extend networks to longer-range routes, or sell their products in more diverse ways. These hybrid airlines have started to outnumber the low-cost carriers. Southwest Airlines is rare among the low-cost carriers, who managed to transform successfully into a hybrid airline by expanding its simple business models steadily and profitably, while keeping its operations efficient and reliable. The impact of different business models on airline punctuality and operating profit margins, works in favour of low-cost carriers on both fronts.

It is obvious that simplified operations create great opportunities for lower cost operation and better on-time performance. But, a few big profitable network carriers are still around, despite their complexities and high rates of disruptiveness. So what kind of model is the best to aim for? According to Richard Koch (Koch 2006, 106): 'because business is wasteful, and because complexity and waste feed on each other, a simple business will always be better than a complex business. Because scale is normally valuable, for any given level of complexity, it is better to have a larger business. The large and simple business is the best.' The only problem is that for most airlines this goal is unachievable.

Many traditional airlines are still adding to an already high level of complexities. When they plan to increase their operations by introducing new routes and frequencies or operating to a new airport, even if this growth is minimal, the disruptions and costs will increase not in proportion with the volume of operation, but well ahead of it. This is because they add to complexity in the way that they create many unknown links that require more of management time to deal with the additional number of people or new gaps in communication. This is the case with continuous traffic expansion at the busiest airports. In 2007, Heathrow airport served about 68 million passengers – 50 per cent over its designed capacity, and no wonder that punctuality continues to deteriorate rapidly year on year. According to British Airways, airport and ATC problems at Heathrow, its base airport, generated the accumulated amount of unproductive time spent in holding, arrival delays and ground movement delays, equivalent to an average of 43.1 hours a day or five grounded British Airways aircraft a day in 2004 (Aerodrome Congestion Working Group 2005, 5). The debacle at the opening of the new Heathrow Terminal 5 in 2008 resulting in cancellation of over 400 flights, only added to an already critical situation with this airport.

Apart from strategic moves towards simplicity through adjustment of business models, both legacy and low-cost airlines should focus on simplification of internal processes and daily practices, where there is always lots of room for improvements. One of the ways to simplify the decision-making processes is to be able to focus on problem areas that are most damaging for airline operational and financial performance. The key is to search for the most critical issues, which once resolved or their negative effects minimised, can ease off the pressure on other problem areas.

## Focusing on Things That Matters Most

If we bury our heads in the sand (delay and accounting reports are good places), refuse to acknowledge the root causes of disruption problems and control them, they will continue to accumulate, generating the unknown increase in operating costs. Each airline, be it low cost, hybrid or legacy carrier, has a certain level of inefficiencies that can be prevented, or their negative effect on cost and on-time performance minimised.

Much of airline success depends on where management attention is directed. There are so many things managers can focus on every day. The time spent on solving the problem that does not bring much value to the organisation is wasted time, and can be, in some cases, qualified as a cause of business disruptions. In order to use their time more efficiently and make decisions that contribute to improvements in airline operational and cost efficiency, managers need to focus on the most critical areas of disruption. They need to make sure that actions at departmental levels are coordinated in line with the company's objectives.

We cannot resolve disruption problems just by looking at a vast number of delayed flights, or trying to act on every disruption that comes our way, however important it may look at that particular moment. Airline executives need to develop criteria to prioritise problems that require their involvement. They may otherwise be drawn into the vicious circle, where despite their immense efforts to reduce disruptions and minimise costs, no improvement will ever be made. Another trap into which executives easily fall is to focus on limited number of functional areas when trying to resolve problems of a wider nature.

We have just seen how powerful the effect of the strategic impact of simplified network and fleet structures has on airline cost and on-time performance. Not many airlines however can take big steps towards simplification of their operating models. There are other possibilities that could be exploited to make smaller but still important overall improvements in airline operational and cost efficiency. It is important to distinguish between actions with strategic, longer-term effects and those taken regularly to keep operations aligned with planned objectives. The more narrow focus requires continuous scanning of critical disruptive situations, actions that people take to resolve them and the change in costs that need to be kept within tolerant levels. But, how difficult is it to keep control over so many disrupted flights?

If we look at the total number of disruptions, or deviations of the originally planned schedule, more than 50 per cent of flights undergo changes from what was planned in annual budgets. This includes zero-reference delays, flight cancellations, route diversions, positioning flights, and flights that have departed on time but their schedule patterns, type of aircraft or aircraft ownership has changed. In addition, what we cannot see in operations reports is the number of pre-planned schedule changes. They also represent deviations from budget plan and distort airline operational and financial results. Their number could be vast and their causes various, such as: market fluctuations, planning errors, scheduling oversights, late aircraft deliveries, omissions in maintenance and crew planning, inadequate airport equipment, changes caused by aircraft damage and many more.

A great number of these flights do not have significant impact on airline results. Consider the case of a major European airline operating 300 disrupted flights a day. The number of critical disruptions that required management attention, such as long delays, cancellations and aircraft replacements, typically takes 5 per cent of planned flights or, 37 flights a day on average (10 out of which are initially disrupted). This number does not look unmanageable for airline of that size, and can lead to an even smaller number of direct and indirect causes of disruptions that need to be periodically examined with a focus on cost and quality criteria. This airline incurred estimated disruption losses of over €600,000 in one year. This example shows that the great majority of disruption costs is generated by a small number of flights and can turn actions for improvement in on-time performance into a manageable disruption control process.

The method for disruption loss management contains the necessary elements to provide instant access to quantitative information of this kind, and supports the analysis of indirect causes, as well as the decision-making processes at various organisational levels. The following are several examples.

Top managers' focus should be on problems of wider scale. They need to ensure that there is a right balance between cost and quality of service whenever the airline experiences bigger deviations in operational patterns. By constantly monitoring overall losses induced by changes in the flying programme, and having first-hand information about disrupted passengers and root causes of disruptions, senior executives will be better equipped to take actions that will resolve not only the obvious problem, but many of the related issues. The focus at operations level may be on repetitive constraints during the departure process, which can develop into bigger problems. Staff awareness about the costs of communication problems that lead to delays, can prevent the operations control centre creating creeping delays just because they keep making over-optimistic predictions about on-time departure times. People at the front line should also be aware of the consequences that their actions have on other processes by looking at the cost of disruptions caused by their failure to follow procedures. Operations managers should focus on processes in need of improvement and ensure that the operational response to disruptions is in line with the company's objectives. Once they know the value of costs associated with operational disruptions, these objectives will become less abstract and will narrow the gap between operational and corporate strategies.

Generally, improvement in disruption management should be coordinated by senior management, who need to be able to directly access information about the worst affected areas of airline operations. Those responsible for finances should constantly monitor overall changes in costs. Whenever delta costs get over the predefined limits, top executives should be able to identify the most critical causes and initiate actions to put costs back within an acceptable framework. If the number of passenger disruptions reached an unacceptable level putting revenue at a higher level of risk, senior managers will be compelled to find out more about causes of problems, evaluate the risk of future losses, decide about operational priorities, and protect the most significant routes from further deterioration in quality of service. A similar approach applies to other processes – maintenance, ground operations, crew planning, and other segmented functions. The most important thing is that all of these activities are well coordinated and based on the information that comes from the same source and can be communicated across the airline.

Apart from focusing on the biggest disruption losses, airlines should try to identify emerging patterns hidden behind frequent, but less costly events. It requires good analytical skills, but the results could be highly rewarding.

Without taking an integrated approach to disruption management, airlines will continue to suffer from failed efforts to focus on isolated improvements in highly interrelated processes. The following case illustrates how a good idea in fighting delays initiated and organised at the operational side, failed to produce longer-lasting effects. A major legacy airline organised a project with the intention to focus on preventing delays on 'critical flights', usually the most important early morning flights that, if delayed, had a ripple effect that could spread all over the system. The ultimate goal was to pull the aircraft away from the gate, ready to take off, about five minutes ahead of schedule. The focus on critical flights called for a coordinated effort among several different employee groups at operations level including gate agents, mechanics, baggage handlers, flight attendants and pilots, as well as some outside contractors such as catering services. The airline claimed that within a year since the introduction of these policies it moved three positions up on the punctuality league table. However, the improvement was short lived as many of the interrelated processes intruded into the operation of the project and there was no one from the corporate level to coordinate these activities.

Choosing the right focus is the key to successful improvement actions. The wide scope of information contained in the system for disruption loss management can help senior managers to use their time most effectively. By obtaining instant access to information about the most disruptive areas of an airline's operation, their costs and causes, decision makers can get answers to a wide variety of questions that may arise. The method for disruption loss control stimulates questioning for which many answers should be provided by drilling through several information layers. This can help to narrow management focus down to the point from which the qualitative information needs to be used to get more close to sources and effects of disruption problems. Isolating problems that matter is important, but in order to monitor the progress in resolving it effectively we need a system for measurement of airline operational efficiency.

**Measuring**

*Objective*

Disruption information provides an opportunity for measuring airline performance by combining elements of operational and financial side of business. Compared with other business measures, this brings a more dynamic insight into the changes in the operational environment. Disruption information organised in the disruption information system enables airlines to measure extensively, from their operational and cost efficiency to exposure to disruption risks, their responsiveness and adaptiveness to changes and much more. Measuring performance through disruptions will also improve planning processes, communication, control, and motivation.

Operational events, delta costs, and disruption causes are the disruption properties that are the bases for the defining of key disruption parameters. Operational events and delta costs are the consequences of past events, while disruption causes reveal past and present system weaknesses that can help shape future actions. Associating the delta cost of disrupted operations with operational events and their root causes opens vast opportunities for measuring and analysing the quality and efficiency of operational performance from many different perspectives.

Measurement determines where management attention is focused. If measurement of disruptions is based on delays, attention is drawn to delays and the operational environment. We have already seen that disruptions are far more than an operational issue and that longer-lasting improvements require performance measurement that can reach to management level. To get their attention, performance measurement needs to expand beyond purely operational parameters and include cost and revenue as an integral part.

Performance measures are the important management tool and should be chosen carefully. By measuring everything, the company is implying that nothing is important, and may spread confusion about its real values. The type of measures an airline introduces sends a message to employees as to what the organisation values most and what they as individuals or departments may be accountable for. As an example, if a scheduling or network planning department is not held responsible for operational performance, people will make little or no effort to better understand how their work affects airline operational performance and costs.

The quality and content of a performance measuring system creates a specific mindset that affects employees' behaviour. If speed prevails over the quality of interaction, people involved in decision making will consciously or subconsciously compromise quality for speed. It is therefore important to have a right mix of measures that support operational, departmental as well as the strategic intentions of an airline. By including operational parameters through events, cost values and their cross-functional origins, the measurement system would be able to fulfil this goal.

When deciding about the scope of the measurement system, airlines need to ensure that time, money and energy invested in creation of performance measurement do not override its true value. It has to be simple and accurate enough to fulfil its objective.

While event and delta costs are disruption parameters that can be measured with a reasonable amount of accuracy, the situation is somewhat different with measuring causes of disruptions, and will be explained in more detail.

*Measuring disruption causes*

As we have seen, most airlines focus their attention on direct causes of delays using the existing coding framework. Managers often distrust the delay coding system considering it as subjective, and sensing that there is much more behind the front-line causes. Still, they do not do much to approach the problem more systematically. For some, using the existing delay codes seems to be sufficient for a very practical reason – to do the 'job' quickly. Not many airlines managed to bridge this information gap successfully.

Coding the disruption causes accurately can have much greater value then using them as a tool to assign responsibilities to individual departments or persons at operations level. Relational causes of disruptions that are responsible for most of operational disruptions and for changes in budget costs are the area of greater interest to the decision makers and strategists at top organisational level. Knowledge about usually hidden causes of changes in airline plans is invaluable information for planners at corporate and departmental levels who have to make numerous compromises while trying to design a cost effective, competitive, and operationally stable product.

Although many of deviations from originally planned operations are inescapable, much of what is considered unmanageable can be controlled if companies properly account for root causes of problems and understand their multi-dimensional character.

Traditional measures of operational performance divide reasons for delays in functional groups (ground operations, maintenance, crew, and so on) so that responsibilities could be traced to the department that is thought to have caused it. Periodical reports of on-time departures are allocated to each department, and that is how their performance is perceived at the top management levels of many airlines. Refusing to see the true causes of disruptions and accept them as a result of interdependent processes, some airline managers unknowingly increase operating costs and contribute to loss of reputation, as in the following example.

The CEO of a big airline was reading the punctuality report that, for the fourth month in a row, showed a significant increase in the number of delays caused by technical reasons. Long delays and cancellations have even started to attract media attention. Shareholders put additional pressure on management to take immediate action. The CEO asked for an urgent report about the problems and received a prompt reply from the maintenance department. Unhappy with this response, he could not resist the temptation to take quick action and demonstrate his willingness to resolve the problem efficiently. He was aware that the company does not have a reliable system to establish the root causes of problems quickly and objectively, and refused to wait for the information to 'harden'. He sacked one of the managers in the maintenance department and caused unintended but harsh impact on employees' morale. The problem was not resolved for some time, and not before the real root causes were identified. They were rooted in other departments and in the failure of responsibilities of senior management, including lack of control of outsourced services, missing interdepartmental procedures, and poor internal communication. It appeared that the wrong person lost his job. During this 'sunk' period the company incurred unnecessary losses, but more importantly, created a distrust between employees and management that took a long time to heal. If the CEO was able to obtain fast information about the true reasons and costs of technical disruptions at the time the first signs of serious problems were spotted, the end of story would be very different.

Different airlines measure delay reasons in different ways, depending on management style, organisation, and the company's culture. There are still carriers that are strict in applying the coded reasons to assign responsibilities for delays to departmental units or individuals. This kind of performance measurement turns the departure process into a race where people are mostly interested in finishing their own assigned task before the others – even if they have to hide information to avoid investigative procedures and blame. In many cases, airlines that use detailed coding and sub-coding systems for delay reasons have no code for some of routine events, so that problems of this kind are allocated to some of the existing codes. In such circumstances, people do not have time to think about common goals, passengers, knowledge sharing, or to show respect for fellow workers. Discussions about personal and departmental responsibilities for delays are often fierce, resulting in conflicts and frequent misidentification of the problem that may seriously affect internal communication or the relationship with service suppliers.

To get around the conflicting process of delay reason coding, some airlines have created alternative ways for performance measurement. The results of study carried out by Jody Hoffer Gittell in her book, *The Southwest Airlines Way*, who compared different approaches to performance measurement of four US airlines – Southwest, American, Continental and United – showed that a cross-functional approach to performance measurement at operational level contributes to the improvements in departure performance, particularly faster turnaround times, greater staffing productivity, fewer lost bags, and fewer customer complaints. The findings are quite interesting despite the passage of time.

American Airlines kept a strict functional approach where every delay is scrutinised. Each time a delay occurs, managers on duty were responsible for figuring out which function caused it. Immediate penalties accompanied delays, in the form of having to explain what happened. This system had the unintended effect of encouraging employees to look out for themselves and avoid recrimination, rather than focusing on their shared goals of achieving high-quality outcomes efficiently.

United Airlines introduced 'families' of delays, so that up to three departments could be held responsible for a given delay, and all are therefore expected to work on finding and resolving the root cause of problems. Another novelty was introduction of measurement of on-time arrivals rather than departures to combine the goals of the station and flight department. According to a Los Angeles customer service manager:

> Individual managers are not responsible for just their own department's delays because we have families of delays now. As a customer service manager, I may be responsible for delays that are partly caused by flight attendants. This means I'm supposed to communicate with that other group. Flight attendants and customer service agents interact a lot. This system makes them talk. It's a family of delays. There is no win or lose.

Continental Airlines limited each delay to be charged to only two departments introducing two levels of causes – primary and secondary – in order to increase the level of shared responsibility. Despite improvements in this area, overall results were undermined by an excessive attention on documenting of what happened and why. According to a station manager of Continental Airlines:

> Barriers between groups – it all comes down to the delay coding system. Upper management just wants to have a tracking system. If you have a lot of code 31s (maintenance delays), and then the maintenance guy is gone, you know it is punitive. That is the bottom line.

> You come in front of the tribunal. Headquarters doesn't have time to look at the details. They just see code 10s and then passenger services has a lot of explaining to do ... It's a punitive system, but you are a good station manager, you buffer it, don't allow it to cascade down to the frontline employees.

Southwest created a culture of more open reporting of problems, instead of insisting on 'precise' information of the cause of delays, and blaming a person for problems of a 'multi-dimensional' nature. In order to diffuse blame culture and stimulate learning, the company has introduced a category of 'team delay', in parallel with 10 other delay categories – much less than other carriers.

There are obviously lots of activities and different approaches in using the direct causes of operational disruptions to alleviate disruptions at operational levels. They are, however, not sufficient to satisfy the needs of managers at higher organisational levels who need to have a deeper insight into the cross-functional causes of disruptions.

Indirect causes of disruptions cannot be measured. Most of them are hidden and many are not even perceived as possible reasons for disrupted operation. Getting to the true causes of disruption is not that difficult for experienced people who understand airline processes, and have a good knowledge about the work and information flows, internal relationships, and the company's culture. This is an important part of the process for disruption loss management. It requires more direct involvement of planners, strategists, and senior managers in strategic aspects of operational problems, which can help establish previously non-existent departmental links that are necessary for more effective management.

*Defining measures*

There is a big flaw in measuring airline business performance. Separation of financial and operational measures makes it hard to understand the origins and magnitude of operational inefficiencies.

All airlines measure operational performance. The majority of operational measures focus on things like employee productivity expressed in RTKs[2] and ATKs[3] per employee, aircraft utilisation, punctuality, and regularity. On the other side, financial performance is measured by volume of traffic revenue and expenditures, operating margins and other financial metrics – their links with operations is through block hours, sectors, RTKs and ATKs among several other operational parameters. It leaves many business questions unanswered and involves lots of subjective judgments and decision making, from operational to strategic.

As we have already seen, existing measures of operational and financial performance cannot help in mitigating the negative effects of operational disruptions. Managers that do not know what are the main causes of disruptive changes in planned operations, and how much money the company loses because it cannot reduce their negative impact, have no chance of improving operational performance. Things can change for the better with the introduction of the system for disruption loss management, where these issues will become more transparent and make it possible for decision makers to identify the root causes of adverse changes. Using these measures will help to attract management attention to the most critical problems at both operational and the business side. They will ensure that improvement actions are addressed to the right people in the organisation, and that the results of these actions are continuously measured.

We will be using the term *operational efficiency* to describe the operational and cost effectiveness of airline performance. The main challenge in measuring operational efficiency is the large number of specialised processes with different, often conflicting requirements. The decisions made at operational level depend predominantly on *operational parameters*. There is not much time to think about cost effectiveness or to understand the consequences of these actions on other

2   Revenue Tonne Kilometres.
3   Available Tonne Kilometres.

parts of organisation. Decisions at high level, however, are driven by *financial results* without knowing what is determining these results. In order to measure system performance, these differences need to be bridged. This could be achieved by combining operational and financial elements related to disrupted operations. This will complement the missing knowledge on both sides and help senior management to make decisions that are better aligned with system objectives like cost and service quality.

Measuring operational efficiency should involve various aspects of airline performance like operations, schedule and network planning, fleet planning, ground operations among others. Senior managers should be able to access initial, firsthand information about sources of loss-making problems that arise at lower organisational levels. Attention can then be generally focused on things that matter most, avoiding wasted time and resources on resolving problems of minor significance.

The traditional approach to measurement that relies on historical comparisons would not be appropriate for the measurement of airline operational performance. The dynamic character of disruptions and their causes makes results achieved over long historical periods inappropriate for comparison. In just one year, an airline can change service provider, replace old aircraft, reduce hub peaks, outsource aircraft maintenance and much more. Each of these changes will significantly affect the number and cost of disruptions in comparison with the previous year, so that comparing these results could be misleading. Instead, airlines need to continuously monitor changes from various angles over shorter periods, such as months, quarters and operating seasons. If multi-dimensional aspects of changes and their dynamics are well understood, together with process interdependencies, airlines will be in a position to make more realistic plans which will result in less disrupted operations.

Performance measures need to be designed with care, as they can affect future airline results, influence staff and management behaviour, and change the company's culture. With this in mind, we shall move to the next step and introduce some of the key measures of airline operational and cost efficiency.

The following are the ideas of how to measure disruptions, or changes expressed through deviation of operational and cost parameters from the reference plan (Table 5.1). They represent some of the indicators that could be obtained from the disruption information system and used for a variety of purposes. Most of them should not be separated as 'operational' or 'financial', or associated to single departments, as their underlying information crosses those boundaries. The examples shown in Table 5.1 are just illustrative of how broad the measuring can go. One of the values of these measures is that they could be sourced from a single system.

**Table 5.1     Disruption measures**

**SYSTEM MEASURES**

| What can be measured | Measuring parameters |
|---|---|
| Disruption rate | Disrupted flights/total number of planned flights |
| Disruption cost rate | Disruption costs/total planned costs |
| Delta cost rate | Delta costs/planned variable costs |
| Cost critical causes of disruptions | Disruption costs per cause above critical threshold |
| Critical cause patterns | Most frequent initial disruptions caused by the same cause |
| Schedule stability ratio | Number of operational events/total number of planned flights |
| Disruption risk priority rating | Allocating risk priority numbers to most critical causes |
| Disruption loss recovery rate | Loss recovered from third parties/total loss caused by third parties |
| Disruption loss reasons | Disruption loss causes prioritised by amount of losses over time |
| Efficiency of schedule recovery | Average cost per operational event |
| Disruption effect on aircraft utilisation | Disruption related block hours/planned block hours |
| Delay cost | Cost of delays related to causes |
| Efficiency of punctuality investment | Delta cost/punctuality investment (punctuality cost) |
| Passenger disruption rate | Average number of passengers on disrupted flight |
| Disruption dispersion coefficient | Number of initially disrupted flights/number of reactionary flights |

**FOCUSED MEASURES**

| What can be measured | Measuring parameters |
|---|---|
| Hub efficiency | Hub cost ratio (hub vs. total disruption costs) |
| | Cost per cause at hub airport (crew, maintenance, suppliers etc) |
| | Average cost per event (delays, cancellations, diversions etc) |
| | Reactionary/initial flight ratio at hub |
| | Average cost per disrupted hub flight |
| | Initial/reactionary cost ratio |
| | Revenue loss, total and per departing flight |

**Table 5.1** *Continued*

|  |  |
|---|---|
|  | Number of claims and compensation costs |
|  | Lost baggage at hub in comparison with total lost baggage |
|  | Cost of tarmac delays |
| Ground safety at hub airports | Number of ground incidents per airport |
|  | Support of safety risk evaluation including disruption risks |
|  | Number and amount of claimed and recovered losses caused by third parties |
| Outsourced services | Direct and indirect costs of aircraft damage |
|  | Number of disrupted flights per service provider |
|  | Loss generated by service provider |
|  | Event structure and costs breakdown reporting in support of compensation claims |
|  | Loss recovery rates |
| Aircraft operational efficiency | Number and cost of disruptions caused by aged aircraft |
|  | Change in utilisation vs disruption costs |
|  | Disruption events and cost caused by lack of spare parts |
| Crew resources | Number of reactionary disruptions caused by crew |
|  | Causes of crew disruptions |
|  | Cost of crew repositioning and other disruption related costs |
| Route analysis | Disruption costs per sector |
|  | Lost revenue per sector |
|  | Disruption causes per sector |
|  | Number of disrupted passengers |
|  | Avoidable causes of disruptions – structure and cost per cause |
|  | Number and cost of disruption related passenger claims and compensations |
| Spare aircraft | Calculation of aircraft time used for schedule recovery |
|  | Support calculation of true value of spare aircraft |
| Hired aircraft capacities | Cost of hired capacities – total, per lessor, sector, replaced aircraft |
|  | Frequency of aircraft hire their costs and reasons |

**Table 5.1**    *Concluded*

| | |
|---|---|
| Schedule recovery | Number of flight cancellations |
| | Cost efficiency of recovery solutions and revenue loss |
| | Comparison of alternative solutions |
| Technical reliability – reactionary effects | Number of initial and reactionary disruptions caused by technical reasons |
| | Cost of initial and reactionary disruptions caused by technical reasons |
| | Cost of disruptions caused by unscheduled maintenance, spare parts etc. |
| Value delivered to passengers | Number of disrupted passengers – long delays, cancellations and diversions |
| | Most affected routes and airports |
| | Passenger compensations |
| | Evaluation of revenue at risk |

Airlines need to select measures that best satisfy their own needs. Key disruption indicators (KDI) that will be used as a measure of operational performance at various levels should not be overburdened with unnecessary measures, as it leads to confusion. The remaining parameters could then be used to answer questions triggered by key indicators.

Measuring operational efficiency by linking elements of airline strategies and day-to-day operations brings to airlines that introduce these principles into their systems of decision making many advantages, among them are:

- Easier communication of objectives and targets across the organisation.
- Common focus on the most critical causes of operational problems.
- Investment initiatives that are better aligned with operational needs.
- More valuable contribution of operations managers to the process of strategic decision making.

The process of disruption loss management is based on simple principles that are required to achieve the goal of improved airline operational efficiency. It starts with asking the right questions and searching for answers by exploring the hard information and then this is followed by using qualitative methods involving experiential knowledge. The results are communicated to people involved in the decision-making process before the final decision is made and action taken. This process is shown in Figure 5.3.

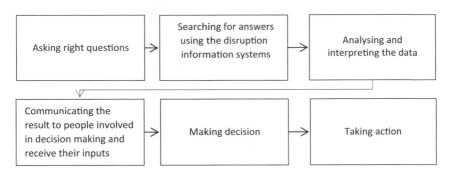

**Figure 5.3    Decision making process**

The following are some of the management questions that could be answered by using the methods for disruption loss management:

- What drivers increase variable costs over the planned values?
- How can cost-saving measures be prioritised and disruptions reduced?
- Why are there so many technical or other more costly disruptions? How much money is at stake? What are the underlying problems?
- How many disruptions were avoidable? What needs to be done? Does it require additional investment, where, and how much?
- What are the effects of outsourced services on the number and cost of disruptions?
- Would investment in more crew/ground equipment help to decrease the number of operational disruptions?
- What is the operational efficiency of individual aircraft?
- How many passengers were affected by delays, cancellations, and diversions, and why? What is revenue loss? How much revenue is at risk?
- How many disruptions are caused by airport operators? Can we claim damage compensations?
- Can we recover the indirect costs of damaged aircraft?

## Organising and Managing Disruptions

*Organising the process*

The process of disruption management relies upon complex interaction across virtually all departments. Managing information about changes in operational performance is a multi-dimensional process that cannot be assigned to individual departments or temporary team members.

Due to its nature, the function for disruption information management needs to be neutral. Those responsible would need to organise and monitor the quality of the

DLM system inputs from all around the airline, but should also be responsible for the 'soft' input, crucial for determining management actions – especially sensitive is the area of root cause analysis and assignment of accountability for disruptions. They would need to cooperate closely with front-line staff, as it is critical that operational data are captured in real time and accurately, but also with the highest organisational level, where company-wide policies and procedures are made. At the same time, they should work closely with individual departments, which can add significant value to this effort through their understanding of local issues.

There are no recipes for how this process should be organised – each airline has to integrate the concept of disruption loss management into its organisation so that it best meets its particular needs. One of the options is to create the central information and communication unit where disruptions related to operational, strategic, network, scheduling and other related problems and information ambiguities could be coordinated, discussed, and whenever possible, resolved. It would consist of 'boundary-spanners' – people who are able to move freely between operations and senior management, translating the requirements of each into a language and behaviour that is acceptable to, and understandable by, the others. 'Boundary-spanners' would have an important role in complex airline structures. They should establish 'experience bridges' that link people, information and process, and accelerate progress through the development of shared understanding. They could prove to be a good investment, considering that the introduction of this function will make significant reductions in time and money spent on unnecessary analysis, unreliable delay reports, futile decision making, and endless disputes over unsolvable problems – time that could be spent more effectively by shifting the focus from fire-fighting to longer-term improvements in operational efficiency. Additionally, gains in punctuality improvement and reduced costs could be achieved as a result of the introduction of this function.

There is another possibility for organising the process of disruption information management that might be appropriate for smaller airlines with flat organisations and those who argue that bringing all information about disruption information management within the scope of a single unit may itself be limiting. For them, the gain from a single functional responsibility may be less attractive than building appropriate procedures into all aspects of disruption management. Even then, system ownership must be clearly defined.

In both cases, it is essential for airlines to have a well-developed disruption information system in place, incorporating the elements explained earlier in this book. It will create a good base upon which other parts of the system could be successfully built. Disruption information delivered from this point through DLM should replace simplistic and unreliable delay reports and make a valuable contribution towards improvement in operational change management.

## *Accountability*

Accountability for disruptions needs to be more clearly identified, and shared between groups of participants involved in the disruption process, including senior managers. There are many examples where measuring operational performance by shared groups of causes positively influences communication and problem solving, improves interdepartmental relationships and the sharing of knowledge with longer lasting effects on operational performance. This kind of measuring should replace the current system where departmental responsibilities for delays are assigned to individual departments and even individuals, on the basis of unreliable information coded in delay reports. This system has proved to lead to the creation of a blaming culture and tends to hide or distort the information. It does not mean that individual responsibilities should be eliminated in case of repetitive errors and omissions. The difference in approach would be that performance measures do not result in punitive measures, but allows people to learn from mistakes and improve over time. The reasons for disruptions measured from various operational and strategic aspects will allow airlines to use experiences based on disruption evaluation and simulate alternative solutions to encourage the learning process and keep best practices in the 'organisational memory'.

## *Communication*

The cross-functional character of disruption management will stimulate management communication with employees at all levels and between departmental units. The better the communication between organisational units, the more knowledge will be shared and fewer problems created at every level: strategic decision makers will be more aware of the effects that their decisions to purchase diverse or aged fleet, or add new generation aircraft to the airline's fleet, will have on maintenance, operations, or crew planning departments. Sales and marketing people will know more about operational limitations and costs, and operations controllers may learn more about marketing and sales priorities. From shared knowledge comes mutual respect. Communication does not just improve the quality and efficiency of service delivery – it improves both simultaneously. These are all elements that can have a profound effect on solutions related to improvements of airline operational performance.

Good communication cannot be built if there is a problem with cross-functional information. The disruption information system that contains operational and corporate elements assembled in one place, can become a point through which internal communication can be enhanced together with the learning process

We have discussed how much lack of communication at functional levels can affect operational performance and create 'companies' within the 'company' although each of them may do brilliant jobs in their own right. A planner can do a brilliant job by drafting more 'profitable' flights and increase aircraft utilisation; the schedule planner can squeeze this plan into the aircraft rotation scheme by cutting the turnaround times, and increase the number of connecting flights; and all this can look like a job well done – the final calculation shows an increase in profit. Detached from their colleagues in front-line departments, who often complain that many parts of the schedule plan are unworkable, planners may interpret front-line requirements as a lack of understanding of 'bigger' issues, and ignore them. This lack of mutual understanding arising from functional detachments are the hidden causes of many disruptions, and are more typical for complex airline organisations.

*Culture*

One of the important things in introducing a system for disruption loss management is the creation of a culture that will support knowledge, trust and communication across the airline. These values need time to develop, but the process could be facilitated by the use of a reliable disruption information system and through people who can spread these values throughout organisation.

One of the hidden causes of disruptions relates to the culture of fear, present in many organisations. Airline staff that work in an atmosphere of constant fear of being blamed for mistakes or from cost cuts and redundancies will hardly show enthusiasm while dealing with disrupted passengers, trying to find the best way to resolve operational problems or entering the right code as the reason for disruptions. This affects the quality of the product and demoralises front-line employees, which can become too visible to the external world. Airline front-line staff control communication with customers. One of their jobs is to keep customers informed when things go wrong. How many times have we seen agents or cabin crew being indifferent or even unpleasant to passengers who experience long delays. At that moment, they do not think that just one inappropriate word may send that passenger to another carrier for another ten years or so.

Everyday work-life shapes people's mindsets as they capture signals from around themselves: the way people work, behave, communicate, spread knowledge, make proposals, are open to express new ideas, are instructed to do things, are impersonating managers' attitudes, secretiveness in vertical communication, investment in things that matter, appreciation of knowledge, embracement of learning culture, no blame policies and much more. Our minds are digesting not only information they can see and hear, but also what we feel, often at unconscious level. The negative signals soon turn a 'fresh' innovator into a silent, obedient worker whose reasoning switches from 'I have a great idea how to improve this thing!' into: 'this requires investment which will mean I will be labelled as a "cost driver", and will cause changes in the way other people work. Because of that, they will not support the idea, and will put additional pressure on my manager who is not going to appreciate this. So, it is more safe to leave things as they are. Further redundancies are on their way and my new mortgage repayment will be in danger. This can improve airline performance, but it is such a trouble – better leave things as they are.' These kind of widespread attitudes are high on the list of hidden disruption causes as they invisibly spread among workers and multiply fast.

A culture of openness, honesty, and cooperation is an important element of improvement in airline performance. Any blockages in information and workflows will affect the results of people that work hard to get the things done. Disruption reporting and resolving inter-related problems depend on the way people are ready to exchange information and communicate.

*Learning*

Managing disruptions require system knowledge and experience – without it, decision makers can themselves become a 'hidden cause' of disruptions. Airlines should encourage learning that will embed knowledge within a person, group, or organisation to help prevent similar problems from recurring in the future. Resolving problems by learning directly from personal experience may not be the cheapest way to enhance knowledge in such a complex area, which includes highly dependent processes. It requires a good understanding of the related workflows within and outside the organisation, the quality of information, and the importance of getting it, and reading it right. People involved in decisions related to changes in operational plans can learn best from disruption information systems that integrate knowledge from around the airline. By constantly analysing major deviations from planned operations, making alternative solutions and looking at similar cases saved in the system 'memory' of scenario builder, managers can get in touch with real life problems through other people's experience. This method can speed up the learning process and stimulate discussions and cross-functional communication. Gaining such knowledge, retaining it, and using it effectively is one of the goals of learning organisations engaged in continuous improvement.

In this and previous chapters we explained the methods that could be useful for streamlining disruptions. The next step would be to describe how best to use the acquired knowledge in practice: how to identify disruption risks and problems beneath the surface, how to cut losses and improve flight punctuality and regularity, and how to use the disruption information system to recover losses caused during disruptions generated by third parties.

# Chapter 6
# Managing Disruption Losses

Disruption loss management is a process that should be ingrained in every part of an airline organisation. Airline operation is the result of the collective effort of every airline member to plan, organise, and deliver a good service to customers. Anything that goes wrong during this process should give an opportunity for learning, and this book is written to contribute to this process.

The method for disruption loss management described in this book can help airline executives to understand why actual operation deviates from business plan, and how much these changes affect the airline's financial results and quality of service. Information contained in a disruption information system reflects the dynamics of changes in operational patterns and related costs, and facilitates the process of true root cause analysis. It turns the purely operational into valuable business information. In order to exploit its full potential, airlines need to organise the process and procedures for disruption loss management with primary objectives to achieve operational excellence. This does not mean eradicating disruptions as it is impossible, but taming them, and being better than competitors in terms of both quality and costs.

The new approach to disruption management is based on integration of its three core elements – operational events, disruption causes, and delta costs – into a single system. Compared with currently used delay information, each of them brings additional value into the process:

- *Operational events* bring together all elements of changes in planned operations, including information about delays, flight cancellations, diversions, additional flights, aircraft type changes and hired aircraft, essential properties necessary for understanding the full effects of disruptions on airline cost, revenue, and passenger service.
- Introduction of *indirect causes* of disruptions expands the knowledge about disruptions beyond the front-line environment, raising awareness about the interrelation of disruption processes and helping with the recognition of true causes of disruptions.
- *Addition of disruption costs* and linked with their causes brings a comprehensive information about changes in planned operations to the attention of senior executives, bridging the gap between strategy and operations.

The comprehensive and reliable information about disruption costs and causes will create opportunities for airline executives to learn more about consequences of operational performance on system results, and allow them to more actively participate in the process of disruption management. They will be able to interpret the information about disruptions in a new way, and make more efficient system decisions. The following are some of the functional areas that can benefit from the introduction of methods for disruption loss control.

## Planning

### Budgeting

Airline budget plans contain funds to absorb possible disruption losses. Some of these costs are hidden behind various cost items in financial reports, like maintenance, aircraft, crew, and fuel among others, and some are included in airline contingency plans. By introducing a system for disruption loss management, this currently obscured information will become more transparent. It allow airline executives to more accurately evaluate operational risks and make more realistic plans for disruption 'allowances'. This process needs to involve planners at corporate level to ensure that risks involved in network, fleet, and schedule plans are realistically projected. Planners and managers will be in position to constantly monitor unforeseen operational changes and make sure that they do not exceed the tolerable cost levels. If they do, the knowledge about disruption origins will allow decision makers to take timely actions to prevent further losses, and channel investment to areas that can improve airline profitability and punctuality.

### Strategies

Creating strategy is one of the most important responsibilities of senior executives. Airlines have changed the way they plan their operations. Long-term forecasts based on macroeconomics, trend extrapolation and other techniques have been replaced with different types of modelling and more frequent reviews of the existing strategies. In this way, airlines are able to predict the future more realistically, in line with fast changes in the increasingly complex environment in which they operate. However, some airlines are confronted with problems which cannot be resolved even with these improved planning techniques and software that do not provide sufficient information about the magnitude of operational losses resulting from inadequate operating models. Consequently, these airlines create strategies that cannot efficiently catch up with operational dynamics, and are exposed to a higher level of operational and financial risk.

The circumstances in which airlines operate are changing more quickly than predicted in annual budget plans, deepening the chasm between plans and reality, resulting in operational disruptions. Many airlines are not well prepared to manage costly changes. The lack of integrated disruption information and organisational inadequacies allow many of the associated problems pass without action. There is a need for transformation in planning dynamics which should be led by a new breed of planners, 'dynamic' strategists rather than traditional ones, whose attempts to predict the future by extrapolating from the past, make the medium- and long-term plans obsolete too soon. The greater the uncertainty and competition, the closer strategies need to be to 'real time'. To manage this gap successfully, executives need to know not only how much the operation has changed, but also why did it change and how much it has cost the airline; answers that could be provided by implementation of a method for disruption loss management. By applying these principles, airlines will be able to plan more realistically and reach a better compromise between numerous conflicting requirements. By accessing synthesised and up-to-date information about the costs of unworkable strategies, they will be able to identify potential for improvement and make timely system adjustments, especially in network and fleet plans that are the main determinants of operational efficiency.

Unforeseen changes are constantly threatening organisations without good strategy. Carefully planned development programmes, with the awareness of past and future disruption risks can help airlines to avoid unpleasant surprises. Instead of waiting for change to happen and then try to catch up with it, airlines should be able to predict changes and be ready for them when they occur.

*Network planning*

The main objective of network planning is to maximise utilisation of the company's assets at the lowest possible costs. Supported by tools for disruption loss management, airlines will have a better insight into various aspects of schedule changes, and be able to more successfully fine-tune tune block-times, scheduling buffers, and ground times with costs, and also, to recognise the elements that can increase the level of disruption risk. Such a complex task is highly dependent on airline operational and financial inputs, and information about available resources of external service providers like airports, ATC and ground handling companies. Without reliable integrated information, network planners will not be in situation to thoroughly and efficiently examine the weakest points of their plans, especially those dependent on links between operational and cost inputs.

One of the biggest challenges for strategists and network planners at legacy airlines is the improvement in efficiency of their hub operations, which are responsible for the majority of operational irregularities and high costs of network airlines that can reach more than one fifth of total operating costs. The problem is that hub-generated disruptions are not just contained within the 'hub' network – they spread widely across the airline system. According to published figures, JFK airport, which in 2007 achieved record low punctuality records in the peak hours, was responsible for 50 per cent of reactionary delays throughout the US. The more intensive the hub operation and the more hubs an airline has, the more the disruptions are generated, driving the cost exponentially higher and quality lower.

To improve the efficiency of this process which involves intensive simulation of disruption scenarios through schedule changes, it is important that all of the necessary hard information comes from the same system. By using the information contained in the system for disruption loss management, network planners will understand, with more certainty, whether the high concentration of disruptions at hub airports is generating returns, or is increasing the company's costs and ruining its reputation. They will be able to more accurately evaluate elements of route and aircraft efficiency, like resource utilisation, schedule-buffer strategies, passenger connection and turn times, and much more, and obtain a better understanding of the true value of their existing network models.

## Fleet planning

Aircraft reliability, utilisation, and fleet structure are among the factors that have a big impact on on-time performance, the number, and type of operational events, and airline costs. The cost of disruptions caused by aircraft-generated problems should be carefully monitored through the disruption information system. This is especially important for network carriers that operate a fleet with multiple aircraft types and crew bases. Airlines with older fleet would be able to measure the 'disruptiveness' and operational losses generated by aged aircraft and see if their replacement with a younger fleet will pay off.

Holding one or more spare aircraft in the fleet could be very costly if airlines do not use these aircraft economically. Many airlines cannot answer the question as to how much having spare aircraft really contributes to improvements in airline punctuality and regularity. The operational and cost efficiency of back-up capacities could become clearer with access to full information about disruptions, including their cost value. Another question that it would be possible to answer with more clarity is the true cost of highly utilised aircraft, which is often covered up by the significant cost of spare aircraft and other resources necessary to achieve competitive on-time performance.

## Schedule planning

In order to plan an efficient and reliable flight schedule, schedule planners go through a long and intensive coordination process with numerous participants within the airline and with external service providers. The complexity of this process often leads to solutions shaped by individual judgements and assumptions. A schedule plan that is based on too many assumptions will lack stability and will become unbalanced even when struck with the smallest operational change. Its impact on operational efficiency could be measured by using the principles for disruption loss management. This system can also provide the information about type, length, cost, and causes of operational disruptions and bring significant improvements to the process of schedule planning. Awareness about operational and cost consequences of disruptions caused by short turn times, peak slots, insufficient maintenance slots, crew planning, or flights planned to operate late to airports with night curfews, can help schedule planners immensely with prioritising during the process of schedule coordination. By sharing the same disruption information with operations, network, crew and maintenance departments among many others, schedule planners will improve communication with major participants in this process, and contribute to a more stable schedule.

*Route planning and pricing*

In order to plan the route network more realistically and price their product competitively, airlines need to understand the dynamics of change in operating costs caused by disrupted flights, and also the quality of service on individual routes. Airlines tend to price their products competitively for each route, while at the same time they do not distribute the costs accurately to each route. Planning techniques, where parts of the planned costs are apportioned down to the route level, are hiding inefficiencies of individual flights. As we have seen earlier, the negative effect of hub operations is huge – it may account for tens or hundreds of thousand dollars of airline expenditures, depending on airline size. If flights operating from congested hubs are among the main generators of disruption costs that spread across the network, but are not identified as the root cause of these disruptions, the results of route cost analyses will be distorted, and may lead to costly strategic errors.

How can the disruption information system help with better route planning and pricing? By being able to allocate disruption losses per sector and understand their relational causes, airlines could be in a position to make more knowledgeable decisions about development of route network, the need for network restructuring, and to better price their products. Information about the volume and cost of disrupted flights can help route planners to better understand the issues related to service quality. They need to be aware about the level of disruptiveness experienced by passengers, like how many passengers had to switch to another carrier, or how much of the revenue was lost due to disrupted services. Apart from having a more accurate information about flight punctuality and regularity, they will be able to have a closer look at how many passengers suffered from long delays, cancellations and diversions, how much the airline spent in passenger compensations, and how much of the revenue was, or could be lost. In addition, they will be able to know if the reasons for disruptions were avoidable, and assess the risk of future recurrences.

Airlines should be able to identify routes that systematically spread reactionary disruptions across the network, associate their costs with the original cause and consider this aspect during the planning process. Equally, they should know what the 'star' performers are – the routes of greatest strategic importance – and prevent them from being disrupted too often.

*Outsourcing*

The majority of airlines that have outsourced previously internal functions, have experienced a significant drop in operational performance, at least during the initial phases, as in the case with Lufthansa and Lufthansa Technik (see Chapter 3, Outsourcing). The consequences of outsourced maintenance and ground handling proved to be the most costly of outsourced services and the most difficult to recover. Management of service level agreements with suppliers is one of the airlines' weak points. The main problem with managing the relationship with suppliers is measurement of actual performance, its causes and consequences. In order to avoid unpleasant and time-consuming disputes, airlines and suppliers need to set criteria about the deadlines for suppliers' process, performance targets, measurement of actual performance and loss recovery, which is where the information contained in the disruption information system can be beneficial. By including these elements in the service level agreement and being more active in monitoring and communicating the results, airlines and suppliers can improve their relationship, reduce cost, and deliver more punctual services.

## Operations

*Operations control*

Airlines are often limited with the choices they can make to resolve operational problems due to restricted, often highly utilised resources, equipment, and infrastructure. On the day of operation, every problem may look important, as it is hard to understand its real value and place in the system. It is understandable that operational decision makers do not have much time to spend on finding the best solution to every operational problem, balancing between cost and quality. As we have mentioned earlier, optimisation tools that could support cost-efficient decisions during schedule recovery are still not as efficient as they should be. Airlines expend a great deal of effort in raising the awareness of operational decision makers about the costs of disruptions, often making simplistic, unproductive assumptions. What else can airlines do to improve operational efficiency in the operations environment?

One of the possibilities is to use the scenario builder as a tool to help airlines with evaluation and comparison of the pre-planned scenarios, and also to analyse recent decisions and compare them with alternative solutions made in the same circumstances. In both cases, decision makers will be in position to learn about cost values associated with their decisions and apply these principles, in combination with experience, in similar situations in the future. This kind of post-flight analysis would be beneficial for schedule and other planners and managers who should occasionally attend the 'sessions' where the same disruptions problem could be seen from various perspectives. This will enhance interdepartmental communication and raise awareness about the magnitude of costs involved in their decisions.

*Crew planning*

Existing management information systems can obscure the extent of crew problems on airline operational or financial results. The full cost generated by crew shortages is not a part of standard operational or financial reports. They may initiate long cascading disruptions and high costs. By separating these costs from other operating costs using the system for disruption loss management, senior managers will get a better understanding of the magnitude of losses caused by insufficient crew. This information could be useful to support the decisions about potential investment in additional crew. Key disruption indicators in the disruption information system will not only signal the changes in crew productivity in operational terms, but will provide information about crew-induced losses that spread throughout the system. More thorough analysis could reveal the crew problems and consequent losses that may reside in strategic, network planning or scheduling departments. One of the examples of consequences of crew shortage on airline operation is described in Appendix 3.

*Maintenance*

Information about the consequences of 'technical' disruptions on system performance shown in traditional reports does not reflect their full effect on stability of flight schedules and impact on operating costs. Majority of the disruption consequences are hidden behind reactionary causes, and may include the high cost of aircraft replacements or additional ferry flights, without being associated with the root cause of disrupted operation.

With support of the DLM, airline executives will be continuously informed about real magnitude of disruption losses caused by technical problems, be it unscheduled repairs, late aircraft release from schedules maintenance, a lack of spare parts or equipment or any other reason. By focusing on the most costly disruptions and being able to get a better insight into their underlying causes, like inadequate spare parts policies, staff shortages, potential organisational, procedural, management and communication issues, or poor quality of outsourced services, managers will be able to take effective actions. In addition, they will be able to learn about problems generated outside the maintenance department, which are responsible for changes in aircraft maintenance schedules.

*Ground operations*

Organisation and coordination of numerous processes related to flight departures and arrivals are highly dependent on synchronised activities of all participants: airlines, airports, ATC, and other service providers. This assumes a well organised work processes, good cross-functional communication stimulated by integrated information, and well trained, disciplined, and highly motivated people. One of the ways to minimise disruption risks related to poor delivery of ground services is by raising management and staff awareness about things that need to be improved, and their impact on operations, processes, and airline costs. In addition, people involved in this process need to understand the value of data input for which they are held accountable. These improvements could be supported by information contained in the disruption information system. Raising awareness about the magnitude of losses involved in disruptions caused by ground services may work more powerfully in reducing disruptions, than incentive schemes linked to the vague delay targets. Furthermore, a new opportunity to measure quality of performance more widely may eliminate the unjust departmental or personal accountability for delay problems of a relational nature. In addition, a disruption information system will allow monitoring and control of services provided by the external service suppliers. It will give managers the power to renegotiate contractual obligations and entitle airlines to damage compensations. More importantly, airlines and service providers can use the comprehensive disruption information to build a better understanding of things that are important, rather than to measure every minute of delay and spend hours or days in disputes about whose responsibility it was.

*Revenue loss control*

Information about revenue that is lost during disrupted operation is among the rare indicators of potential decline in passenger loyalty. These values may not be high, partly because some of the data will not be easy to gather, and partly because not many passengers decide to claim compensation. This does not mean that they will forget the bad experience and remain loyal. The disruption information system will be able to provide much of this information. The complexities related to its systematic collection can be overcome by focusing on the small number of highly and regularly disrupted flights which should be constantly monitored. Current difficulties in accessing this valuable information forced many airlines to look for alternative ways of tackling this problem. The following example described in Ian Ayres's book '*Super Crunchers*' illustrates an original approach of Continental Airlines to minimise negative effects of disruptions on their passengers.

'Kelly Cook, director of customer relationship management, used the coin-flipping approach to figure out how to build stronger customer loyalty. She wanted to see how best to respond when a passenger experienced what Continental euphemistically called a 'transportation event'. This is the kind of event you don't want to experience, such as having your flight severely delayed or cancelled.

Cook randomly assigned Continental customers who had endured transportation events to one of three groups. For the next eight months, one group received a form letter apologizing for the event. The second group received the letter of apology and compensation in the form of a trial membership in Continental's President's Club. And the third group, which served as control, received nothing.

When the groups were asked about their experience with Continental, the control group that didn't receive anything was still angry. 'But the other groups' reaction was amazement that a company would have written them unsolicited to say they were sorry', Cook recalls. The two groups that received a letter spent 8 per cent more on Continental tickets in the ensuing year. For just the 4,000 customers receiving letters, that translated to extra revenue of $6 million. Since expanding this program to the top 10 per cent of Continental's customers, the airline has seen $150 million in additional revenues from customers who otherwise would have had a good reason to look elsewhere.

Just sending a letter without compensation was enough to change consumer perceptions and behaviour. And the compensation of trial membership itself turned into a new source of profit. Thirty per cent of customers who received a trial membership in Continental's President's Club decided to renew their membership after a trial period expired.'

### Disruption Risk Management

Airlines often associate disruption risk with disasters rather than avoidance of costly 'business' mistakes like poor forecasting or investment decisions, and many other factors described as indirect causes of disruptions. This has pushed a number of major airlines into serious financial troubles and has often caused significant loss of competitive position. High competitiveness is wiping out airline 'safety nets', that is the space built into airline plans to cater for inefficiencies. In addition, relentless cost cuts of workforce have narrowed this 'breathing' space even more, increasing the risk of disruptions.

The process of disruption risk management is frequently too narrow and reactive. In too many instances, management emphasis is traditionally focused on contingency planning for recovery from massive disruptions rather than avoidance of costly business mistakes. Management systems and processes aimed at minimising disruption risks are designed mainly around the operational, rather than the corporate level. Managing disruptions risk depends on balancing two strategic goals – quality and cost. They can be controlled only if the costs of disruptions are quantified and responsibilities are clearly assigned.

The system for disruption loss management can provide the information about basic elements for identifying business risks associated with disruptions. This will enable airline managers to work not only on prevention, but also to assess their magnitude and set aside funds to cover for potential losses caused by disruptions. To manage risk properly, airlines must first understand what disruption risk they are taking. To do so, they need to make all of the major financial risks transparent and to define the types and amounts of risks they are willing to take, as in the case of airline strategic decisions to expand hub operations, operate old aircraft, or add additional aircraft type to its fleet. They should also understand how the risks affect different departments and what actions they need to take to make the overall risk minimal.

The importance of quantifying operational risk is quite obvious. However, how these results will be interpreted and used will very much depend on qualitative factors. They are crucial in shaping the choices that relate to the characteristics of the underlying data. Only management experience and judgement supported by tools for disruption loss management can help limit disruption losses.

The traditional approach of airlines has been to tolerate disruption losses – to see it as a cost of being in airline business. Airlines do take actions to reduce operational risks, but they do it in an ad hoc way, with responsibility downloaded to front-line management who, by themselves, cannot do much to avoid disruptions caused by system issues. Goals proclaimed in business plans are difficult for people to translate into their immediate daily tasks. What happens is that rather than taking pre-planned actions to prevent disruptions which in many cases can work, the focus has typically been on controlling problems when they appear.

The difficulty with calculating disruption risks as a part of business risk evaluation is in the way the loss information is structured. If, for example, hub-related losses including lower resource utilisation and overall productivity were consistent for years, the airlines would simply factor these 'expected losses' into their business plans and pricing and not consider them as risk. It is essential that apart from risk of unexpected changes in operational losses, expected losses caused by major drivers of disruptions are included in disruption risk evaluation.

The kind of analysis supported by the system for disruption loss management is more likely to cut losses at source than are the top-down methodologies, or the subjective scoring of various groups or management. While this quantitative data can prove valuable, it is much more difficult, but not impossible, to link an operational risk to specific behaviour and practices in business lines and so to change airline behaviour. The qualitative information gained through the analysis of indirect causes of disruption losses may be used as a corrective factor to hard numbers, which linked to areas of specific risks will allow managers to set the budget price for inefficiencies more accurately. The combination of quantitative and qualitative information will work better with time and will become a reliable foundation for disruption loss evaluation.

The disruption loss evaluation methodology can help the airline to model the likely impact and frequency of operational loss events in various circumstances. This is especially important for assessment of changes in the acceptable level of risk. In addition to this approach, airlines should use saved operational scenarios in 'scenario builder' to estimate the size or frequency of possible operational losses, and make adjustments using a wider set of forward- looking data such as key disruption indicators and disruption loss assessment.

Key disruption indicators include measurable indicators of operational exposures to losses that are strongly linked with the potential for future operational losses, such as the proportion of disruptions associated with airports, fleet or network bottlenecks. These activities should be supplemented with qualitative evaluation at departmental levels.

The conceptual model for evaluation of disruption loss management, as well as tools for assisting executives in improving control of disruption risk, were described in Chapter 4. An example of the quarterly result of disruption risk evaluation carried out by a medium size European airline is shown in Figure 6.1. It shows values of departmental risks complemented with improvement rate indicators.

Though still somewhat subjective, the use of consistent and comparable cross-functional measures of airline exposure to disruption risks would allow airlines to set measurable targets and act to minimise disruption losses. It is important to know that by using cross-functional measures, we are assessing risks without owners, which is why it is essential to involve a broad community that includes experts and all those that might feel the disruption implications.

## Managing Through Disruptions

From management perspective, the main value of principles for disruption loss management is in system simplification with a controllable level of information accuracy, and the possibility for airline executives to identify causes of the cost critical problems. This system is based on criteria that need to be set at strategic

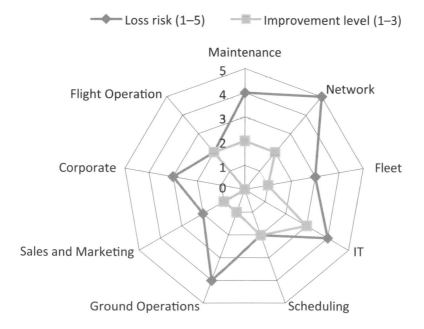

**Figure 6.1    Disruption risk evaluation chart**

and operational levels, in line with airline objectives. Such input includes various parameters related to cost, revenue loss and quality of service, and a set of threshold values from which executives will be alerted to act. With attention focused on things that matter most, executive managers will act more efficiently and be directly in touch with operational aspects of the business, but not immersed in problems that do not merit their attention.

By scrutinising just one major disruption guided by the methods explained in this book, airline executives would be able to learn about the majority of organisational, managerial, cultural, inter-departmental, and a whole range of other internal issues that they would otherwise not be aware of. This insight can be even more important than highly accurate information about losses involved in this event. The example described in Appendix 5 shows how quickly and deeply it is possible to get to the core of underlying disruption problems by following the root causes and costs of major incidents. The findings in this example may look too harsh, but they are true and, if I may say, the majority of situations from this case will not be unfamiliar to many airlines. They illustrate how widespread are the causes of operational disruptions and how wrong it is to search for disruption causes by just looking at disruption codes. By applying this principle whenever the situation allows, managers will be able to take targeted improvement actions and shift their attention to other critical areas as the situation changes.

The difficulties in managing disruptions arise from their complexity, functional and information detachment. One of the major obstacles is created by problems in interdepartmental communication. During the planning process, airlines have to reach consensus among a great number of internal and external participants – the greater the disagreement among them, the higher the level of disruptiveness. Management task would be to create an atmosphere of thrust and cooperation, and ensure that disputable problems are resolved in airline's best interest. A reliable, objective, hard information contained in DLM could support this endeavours.

Airlines can manage strategic issues of disruptiveness by being more systematic and insisting on a high degree of communication to identify various aspects of disruption problems, involve different departments in creating future scenarios and gain wider acceptance for possible strategies. The aim should be to create a shared understanding of the problem and promote a joint commitment to possible ways of resolving it. Not everyone has and will agree on the root causes of problems, but those involved should be able to understand each other's point of view, and so enable them to freely express their own views about the problem solutions, and work together to resolve them.

Executives must go beyond just looking at facts and opinions obtained from departments; departments need to be more actively involved in finding the best solutions to the disruption problems. Seeing the interrelated problems from different perspectives enhances the collective knowledge, neutralises the harmful effects of solutions based on individual judgements, and enables dealing with disruptions more effectively and creatively from a consensus view. Alternatively, in order to avoid the complexities that sometimes may be associated with group work, modern methods of communication could be established by using virtual interaction via intranet, in the form of blog-based discussions.


**Cost Cutting**

One of the most important management functions is to monitor changes in operating costs, understand their causes, and take actions to minimise their negative impact. How can this be achieved by using the methods for disruption loss management? To take a simple example, let us imagine that an airline executive noticed that the airline's operating costs went up 5 per cent above budget. He has read the financial report and traffic results and has noticed that several cost items have gone above plan, but first, he cannot say if this is the result of poor planning or some other reasons, and second he cannot make a reasonable connection between the increase in costs and changes in operations. He has asked his planners to dig through the data and try to find the answers. Some came back saying that this is not really possible as much of the essential information is lost or has never been captured. Others took more time to 'harden' the hard data, make some estimates and came up with conclusions that are 'politically' correct in current circumstances. The thing is, he does not trust this information. What will he do to make sure his actions are heading in the right direction? Let us look at the new approach to disruption loss management and try to find more specific answers to his question.

The first step for him would be to identify the highest disruption losses and their primary causes. His particular focus is on the last quarterly result. We can see from Table 6.1 that 66 per cent (€34,000,000) of disruption costs were caused by 21 per cent of disruption events caused by technical and crew problems alone. And this is where his attention needs to go.

Filtering the information that matters is one of the key elements in prioritising management decisions. It will simplify the process of disruption control and assure that management time is used most effectively. Comprehensive information about disruptions contained in the system for disruption loss management will allow decision makers to get answers to a wide variety of questions.

There are many activities preceding the decision to change the flight schedule and to report on reasons for these changes. The resulting 'hard' information is an anchor and the first step in search for answer about disruption origins and their cost consequences. In this example, the 'crew' and 'technical' reasons appear to be the most frequent and the most costly causes of operational changes. The longer they hold this position, the more thoroughly they need to be scrutinised with support of the DLM system in order to identify their underlying causes. It is normally found that the reasons for the increase in costs are multiple and that some of them are not measurable, like breakage of communication links, insufficient involvement of senior managers in resolving disruption problems, inadequate training, or poor decision-making. It often appears that working on improvements in these areas can be more rewarding than eliminating some of the ad hoc problems, which are

**Table 6.1    Identifying cost critical reasons for disruptions**

| Disruption reasons | Cost | Cost % | Cumulative cost % | Initial events | Events % | Cumulative events % |
|---|---|---|---|---|---|---|
| Technical | 22,000,000 | 43% | 43% | 22 | 10% | 10% |
| Crew | 12,000,000 | 23% | 66% | 24 | 11% | 21% |
| Aircraft | 9,000,000 | 17% | 83% | 41 | 19% | 40% |
| ATC | 5,600,000 | 11% | 94% | 62 | 28% | 68% |
| Ground | 3,200,000 | 6% | 100% | 71 | 32% | 100% |
| Total | 51,800,000 | 100% | | 220 | | |

outside airline control and will reoccur anyway. Meeting these challenges equipped with knowledge, and in supportive environment where people continually work together, is the best way to cope with uncertainties. Even if the airline is not at the top of the punctuality league table, but disruption costs were reduced, this in itself is a success: this may be the result of a decreased number of cancelled flights and that the number of subchartered and spare capacities is less than in the previous year.

Managers who are able to get an insight into the most critical areas of operational and financial underperformance would be able to make better cost-saving decisions. Much of the answers to questions like where to cut costs and where to increase 'productive' costs in order to reach the company's objectives, could be found through information contained in the system for disruption loss management. The quality of this system should be measured by the number of 'why' questions that it could answer.

Methods for disruption loss management encourage 'invest to save' strategies. By associating disruption losses with their root causes, it would be possible to prioritise investments in a more effective way. Investing in prevention of the most risky disruption events can help improve stability of airline schedules and provide valuable returns.

## Loss Recovery

A busy operational environment and an increased number of outsourced services make airlines more susceptible to losses caused by third parties. This may result in extremely high damages that can seriously affect airline operations.

Aircraft damage incidents could put the plane out of service for days or even months. Apart from the direct cost of aircraft damage associated with aircraft repair, it often incurs much higher indirect losses caused by unserviceable aircraft and loss of airline reputation.

While losses above the deductable insurance values can be recovered for direct damages, as well as a part of 'straight' indirect cost like hired replacement aircraft, those below highly set deductibles ($1 million for wide body aircraft) must be borne solely by the airline, unless protective contractual clauses are agreed with the third party.

Despite huge losses generated by incidents caused by third parties, airlines do not have instruments for recovering these losses. Many of their claims are being rejected by insurance companies and by third parties due to a lack of credible evidence about indirect costs of reactionary disruptions. These problems could be overcome with support of the reliable loss recovery system that should be recognised across the airline industry. By applying specific methods for keeping each individual case protected from the influence of non-related disruption costs, airlines can create a credible system that could be used across the industry.

By introducing the system for calculation of indirect losses of damages caused by third parties, airlines would be able to:

- Establish a platform for system savings through the decreased number of incidents and from loss recovery.
- Create credible documentation for indirect loss recovery from third parties.
- Prioritise investments in incident prevention (staff, training, equipment, infrastructure) and increase cost awareness among management and staff.
- Introduce loss recovery clauses in third-party agreements.
- Speed up the legal processes and decrease legal charges.
- Aid auditing processes.

Examples shown in Appendix 6 illustrate the results of loss calculation for two aircraft-damage incidents. The calculations were carried out with the support of a tool based on the principles for disruption loss management. It illustrates the most frequent situations, where indirect costs of aircraft damage are several times higher than direct costs. With detailed evidence recorded with support of scenario builder (described in Chapter 4), airlines would be able to recover much of indirect losses associated with aircraft damage and other third-party damages.


## Quality Control

On-time performance and flight regularity are among the most important components of quality of an airline service with direct implications on future revenue. Still, the function of quality control is mainly focused on individual processes rather than on system issues, which is necessary for real improvements. This process could be supported with information contained in the disruption information system. For some airlines, these activities might be related to the traditional territory of quality control, while for others they may extend well beyond this territory.

**Managing Disruptions Across the Industry**

While trying to achieve their own goals in difficult business circumstances, airlines sometimes put aside the fact that they are only a part of wider socio-economic and natural environment and that the way they operate could have a big impact on peoples' lives. The same applies to other participants in the air transport system, including airports and ATC. The high number and length of ever-increasing flight disruptions indicate serious weaknesses in the air transport system. Years' long warnings by experts that unsynchronised system expansion cannot last forever, and that the existing system has its limitations, seem to reach the critical point when politicians have to become involved to resolve the highly risky delay issues. When the number of flight delays cross that critical line they turn from being just annoyance to people, to something much more serious. In May 2008, the Report of the Joint Economic Committee (JEC) of the US Congress revealed a detailed picture about the effects of flight delays on airlines, passengers and the economy: delays cost the nation's economy in wasted fuel, rescheduled business meetings, and lost productivity $41 billion in 2007 alone, excluding international traffic. Here are some more details from this report:

- Airlines spent $19 billion in fuel, labour and maintenance costs while aircraft sat idle or circled in holding patterns above congested airports (delays wasted 740 million gallons of jet fuel, the price of which has surged in the past year).
- Delays cost passengers about $12 billion in lost productivity and missed business opportunities, connections and pre-paid hotel stays, according to the committee's report. Passengers on domestic flights endured 320 million hours of delays in 2007.
- Hotels, retailers and other companies dependent on air travel for supplies or customers lost $10 billion, the report said.
- Of the 10 million domestic scheduled passenger flights analysed, the JEC found that delays accounted for 19.5 per cent of total flight time, measuring from scheduled departure to actual arrival.
- Planes arrived later than scheduled arrival by more than a total of 2.7 million hours.

The situation regarding the number of flight delays is actually much worse. A large number of delays have become standard at the busiest airports and airlines have adjusted their published schedules to account for predictable delays. In this way, more than half of delayed departures are not shown in delay reports, obscuring the real picture about airline and system efficiencies.

These data were based on the best industry estimates (methods described by JEC), but have revealed many weaknesses in the information system about flight disruptions. While these numbers may call for a higher level of government involvement, improvements in the air transport system seems to be years away.

It will not happen before airlines start to recognise the true value of damages caused by disruptions, to passengers and the economy. The airline industry needs a standardised framework for disruption management, with special attention on identifying the true causes of disruptions. As we have seen, an airline cannot expect things to improve before all parts of the wider system work harmoniously. Better coordination between airlines, airports, and ATC is a precondition for improvement in the efficiency of the air transport system. Among actions that could speed up this process is the creation of standards for disruption measurement at industry level, which could lead to introduction of a new disruption categorisation system for airlines and airports.

### Who Cares About Passengers – A Regulatory Experience

Whenever administrative measures intrude into the business environment, they indicate that there is something wrong within the industry, something that cannot be resolved by companies themselves. This was the case with the EU legislation on protection of disrupted passengers, which raises the question: who really cares more about passengers – airlines or governments? Or, how effectively can the administrative measures help resolve the deeply rooted disruption problems? The following example may help answer this questions.

In the beginning of 2005, the European Union introduced a controversial EC Regulation No. 261/2004 aimed at establishing common rules on compensation and assistance to air passengers in the event of denied boarding, cancellations, and long delays. The originally good intention of the regulator to better protect passengers, encourage healthy competition, improve services, and harmonise national legislations has been distorted along the way, resulting in a highly disputable and unworkable framework for passenger protection and for the industry in general.

The Regulation was harshly criticised by airlines and described as ambiguous, confusing, ill-conceived, discriminatory, and damaging to the industry. In addition, the regulator has been accused of infringement of balanced and democratic procedure and in breach of international law. Airlines have described the legislation as deeply flawed, and potentially very damaging not only to their businesses, but also to their relationship with customers. The Regulation has been legally challenged in the European Court of Justice by airline organisations representing more than 300 airlines, but without success.

Passengers experiencing disruptions have faced difficulties in settling their disputes with airlines under the new rules. The consumer watchdog and designated national complaint body in the UK, the Air Transport Users Council (AUC), claimed they may try to help, but had no powers to compel service providers to accept their views. The AUC's competence in resolving the highly complex regulatory issues has already been questioned during the consultation period, as well as their credibility in protecting passengers while continuing to be funded by airlines.

Passengers who decide to pursue their compensation claims further through Small Case Courts and other legal chains have a little chance of succeeding whenever the evidence of compliance with the provisions of the EC Regulation is non-existent. The lack of clarity in the Regulation makes it difficult, if not impossible, in setting binding legal parameters.

The whole concept of compensating passengers in cases of cancellations and denied boarding was based on the misconception that airlines can provide reliable information on causes of flight disruptions. The Department for Transport's consultation paper on proposed enforcement Regulations in the UK revealed that much of the information that would need to be kept is not currently held by airlines, giving the government no choice but to enforce the EC Regulation with a 'light regulatory touch'. To make things even more confusing, the regulator introduced the term 'extraordinary circumstances' as a reason for flight disruptions out of airline control, for which they are not liable to compensate passengers. In the absence of a clear definition of 'extraordinary circumstances', the regulator has allowed individual airlines to decide if and when they will offer compensation to passengers. Some airlines have chosen to openly declare technical and airport related problems as factors out of their control. The majority, however, have abstained to do so publicly.

While it was obvious that the flawed Regulation could not improve flight punctuality and regularity, nor better protect passengers, it has most certainly incurred additional cost for airlines. The magnitude of these costs is hard to evaluate. According to the estimate made by the European Regions Airline Association (ERA), the full implementation of the new legislation has added €1.5 billion per year to the already high costs of airline operations. This estimate made during the consultation period will probably never be realised, as many of the Regulation's clauses are simply not enforceable

Several years on, and the number of disrupted passengers is still increasing, with little prospect of passengers receiving the 'promised' compensation, apart from those that airlines already offer to their passengers. Despite the fact that disruptions could be caused by the external factors, the legislation holds airlines responsible for passenger delays and flight cancellations, It suggests that airlines could take further steps in recovering their costs from service providers including airports, ATC or other parties that caused the disruptions in the first place. Obviously, the Regulation has only aggravated and not resolved the underlying industry problems which are closely related to the issues explained in this book. In order to be resolved, they require much wider action and coordinated efforts at industry level.

# Conclusions

It was about three decades ago when airlines started to increase block times as an answer to the growing number of operational disruptions. This process continued for almost two decades at an accelerating pace. Increased inefficiencies resulted in an even higher number of flight disruptions. During this period, traditional airlines had their ups and downs, but people continued to travel more and pay more for more disrupted services. However, towards the end of the 1990s and the beginning of the 2000s, things started to change significantly with the emergence of low-cost carriers. They proved that it is possible to operate more efficiently with lower costs. This new concept of flying has knocked travel prices down and improved flight punctuality – exactly what the majority of passengers wanted. Many traditional airlines operating expensive hub networks have become synonymous with high costs and poor punctuality. Disruptions at major hub airports have reached alarming levels. The administrator of the Federal Aviation Administration (FAA) in the US explained the state of the transportation system in 2007: 'We are at a breaking point.' Flight delays have reached a record high, and they are expected only to worsen. The situation in Europe is also becoming critical at the most congested airports. With no system solution in sight, airlines need to turn to exploit their hidden internal potential in order to increase their operational efficiency. Better understanding, management, and control of operational disruptions will surely support these endeavours.

Disruptions 'produce' a lower quality of service, require more block time, more aircraft, more crew, more fuel, more stands, more equipment – always pushing costs up and service quality down. To get to grips with disruptions, airlines must have the system in place to identify, measure and analyse causes and costs of operational changes and then to work on their improvements, control and standardisation. By gaining a deeper insight into the problems associated with disruptions, airline executives will be in a better position to identify the size of the gap between airline plans and reality and take actions to make that gap as small as possible. Disruptions need to be constantly reviewed to make certain that they are in line with costs in money and time, and that there is sufficient number of competent people to do the job. Airlines should never stop focusing on disruptions. Punctuality is important, but is only a part of the picture of airline operational efficiency. Improvements will last only if the process of disruption loss control is integrated in airline daily practices and is at the top of management agenda.

It is important to remember that disruption loss management is a process of discovery. Airlines need to keep reinventing their own capabilities to get an edge on competitors and create new opportunities for growth. Whether they are using the system for disruption loss management to save costs, make targeted investments in punctuality, or increase revenue, airlines should constantly question how they could deploy the DLM principles in a new way to enhance the overall performance.

Airlines may face resistance while confronting the disruption problems that can reveal their internal weaknesses, especially at higher organisational levels, but this should not prevent them from doing so. Facing the full effects of schedule changes is important, as otherwise airlines will never effectively address the true origins of the loss making problems beyond disruptions, and will continue to live in an obscured world of disruptiveness that create inefficiencies, losses and poor service quality.

There is so much to be learned from flight disruptions. They offer us invaluable information about business failures that can be improved. Deviations from originally planned operations could teach us how to accept, manage, and control changes, and how to create links between strategy and operations. Knowledge about disruptions inspires new ideas and leads to departure from traditional thoughts. Introduction of methods for disruption loss management will open the door for transformation of chaotic and uncoordinated change decisions into a consciously controlled disruption loss management. It will generate new opportunities for cost saving, and improvements in quality of service to customers, with less delays and cancellations. Although the process is not as straight and as fast as cutting the labour costs, the result will be much more rewarding and longer lasting.

'I used to think that running an organisation was equivalent to conducting a symphony orchestra. But I don't think that's quite it; it's more like jazz. There is more improvisation.'

Warren Bennis

# Appendices

# Appendix 1
# Standard IATA Delay Codes

**Free Airline Coding**

00–05 AIRLINE INTERNAL CODES

06 (OA) NO GATE/STAND AVAILABILITY DUE TO OWN AIRLINE ACTIVITY

09 (SG) SCHEDULED GROUND TIME LESS THAN DECLARED MINIMUM GROUND TIME

**Passenger and Baggage**

11 LATE CHECK-IN, acceptance after deadline

12 LATE CHECK-IN, congestions in check-in area

13 CHECK-IN ERROR, passenger and baggage

14 OVERSALES, booking errors

15 BOARDING, discrepancies and paging, missing checked-in passenger

16 (PS) COMMERCIAL PUBLICITY/PASSENGER CONVENIENCE, VIP, press, ground meals and missing personal items

17 (PC) CATERING ORDER, late or incorrect order given to supplier

18 (PB) BAGGAGE PROCESSING, sorting etc

**Cargo and Mail**

21 (CD) DOCUMENTATION, errors etc

22 (CP) LATE POSITIONING

23 (CC) LATE ACCEPTANCE

24 (CI) INADEQUATE PACKING

25 (CO) OVERSALES, booking errors

26 (CU) LATE PREPARATION IN WAREHOUSE

27 (CE) DOCUMENTATION, PACKING etc (Mail Only)

28 (CL) LATE POSITIONING (Mail Only)

29 (CA) LATE ACCEPTANCE (Mail Only)

**Aircraft and Ramp Handling**

31 (GD) AIRCRAFT DOCUMENTATION LATE/ INACCURATE, weight and balance, general declaration, pax manifest, etc

32 (GL) LOADING/UNLOADING, bulky, special load, cabin load, lack of loading staff

33 (GE) LOADING EQUIPMENT, lack of or breakdown, e.g. container pallet loader, lack of staff

34 (GS) SERVICING EQUIPMENT, lack of or breakdown, lack of staff, e.g. steps

35 (GC) AIRCRAFT CLEANING

36 (GF) FUELLING/DEFUELLING, fuel supplier

37 (GB) CATERING, late delivery or loading

38 (GU) ULD, lack of or serviceability

39 (GT) TECHNICAL EQUIPMENT, lack of or breakdown, lack of staff, e.g. pushback

**Technical and Aircraft Equipment**

41 (TD) AIRCRAFT DEFECTS

42 (TM) SCHEDULED MAINTENANCE, late release

43 (TN) NON-SCHEDULED MAINTENANCE, special checks and/or additional works beyond normal maintenance schedule

44 (TS) SPARES AND MAINTENANCE EQUIPMENT, lack of or breakdown

45 (TA) AOG SPARES, to be carried to another station

46 (TC) AIRCRAFT CHANGE, for technical reasons

47 (TL) STAND-BY AIRCRAFT, lack of planned stand-by aircraft for technical reasons

48 (TV) SCHEDULED CABIN CONFIGURATION/VERSION ADJUSTMENTS

Damage to Aircraft & EDP/Automated Equipment Failure

51 (DF) DAMAGE DURING FLIGHT OPERATIONS, bird or lightning strike, turbulence, heavy or overweight landing, collision during taxiing

52 (DG) DAMAGE DURING GROUND OPERATIONS, collisions (other than during taxiing), loading/off-loading, damage, contamination, towing, extreme weather, conditions

55 (ED) DEPARTURE CONTROL

56 (EC) CARGO PREPARATION/DOCUMENTATION

57 (EF) FLIGHT PLANS

**Flight Operations and Crewing**

61 (FP) FLIGHT PLAN, late completion or change of, flight documentation

62 (FF) OPERATIONAL REQUIREMENTS, fuel, load alteration

63 (FT) LATE CREW BOARDING OR DEPARTURE PROCEDURES, other than connection and standby (flight deck or entire crew)

64 (FS) FLIGHT DECK CREW SHORTAGE, sickness, awaiting standby, flight time limitations, crew meals, valid visa, health documents, etc

65 (FR) FLIGHT DECK CREW SPECIAL REQUEST, not within operational requirements

66 (FL) LATE CABIN CREW BOARDING OR DEPARTURE PROCEDURES, other than connection and standby

67 (FC) CABIN CREW SHORTAGE, sickness, awaiting standby, flight time limitations, crew meals, valid visa, health documents, etc

68 (FA) CABIN CREW ERROR OR SPECIAL REQUEST, not within operational requirements

69 (FB) CAPTAIN REQUEST FOR SECURITY CHECK, extraordinary

**Weather**

71 (WO) DEPARTURE STATION

72 (WT) DESTINATION STATION

73 (WR) EN ROUTE OR ALTERNATE

75 (WI) DE-ICING OF AIRCRAFT, removal of ice and/or snow, frost prevention excluding unserviceability of equipment

76 (WS) REMOVAL OF SNOW, ICE, WATER AND SAND FROM AIRPORT

77 (WG) GROUND HANDLING IMPAIRED BY ADVERSE WEATHER CONDITIONS

**ATFM + AIRPORT + GOVERNMENTAL AUTHORITIES**
**AIR TRAFFIC FLOW MANAGEMENT RESTRICTIONS**

81 (AT) ATFM due to ATC EN-ROUTE DEMAND/CAPACITY, standard demand/capacity problems

82 (AX) ATFM due to ATC STAFF/EQUIPMENT EN-ROUTE, reduced capacity caused by industrial action or staff shortage, equipment failure, military exercise or extraordinary demand due to capacity reduction in neighbouring area

83 (AE) ATFM due to RESTRICTION AT DESTINATION AIRPORT, airport and/or runway closed due to obstruction, industrial action, staff shortage, political unrest, noise abatement, night curfew, special flights

84 (AW) ATFM due to WEATHER AT DESTINATION AIRPORT AND GOVERNMENTAL AUTHORITIES

85 (AS) MANDATORY SECURITY

86 (AG) IMMIGRATION, CUSTOMS, HEALTH

87 (AF) AIRPORT FACILITIES, parking stands, ramp congestion, lighting, buildings, gate limitations, etc

88 (AD) RESTRICTIONS AT AIRPORT OF DESTINATION, airport and/or runway closed due to obstruction, industrial action, staff shortage, political unrest, noise abatement, night curfew, special flights

89 (AM) RESTRICTIONS AT AIRPORT OF DEPARTURE WITH OR WITHOUT ATFM RESTRICTIONS, including Air Traffic Services, start-up and pushback, airport and/or runway closed due to obstruction or weather1, industrial action, staff shortage, political unrest, noise abatement, night curfew, special flights

**Reactionary**

91 (RL) LOAD CONNECTION, awaiting load from another flight

92 (RT) THROUGH CHECK-IN ERROR, passenger and baggage

93 (RA) AIRCRAFT ROTATION, late arrival of aircraft from another flight or previous sector

94 (RS) CABIN CREW ROTATION, awaiting cabin crew from another flight

95 (RC) CREW ROTATION, awaiting crew from another flight (flight deck or entire crew)

96 (RO) OPERATIONS CONTROL, re-routing, diversion, consolidation, aircraft change for reasons other than technical

**Miscellaneous**

97 (MI) INDUSTRIAL ACTION WITH OWN AIRLINE

98 (MO) INDUSTRIAL ACTION OUTSIDE OWN AIRLINE, excluding ATS

99 (MX) OTHER REASON, not matching any code above

*Source:* Provisional list composed by IATA (Published by: Eurocontrol)

# Appendix 2
# Resolving the 'Technical' Delay

Operational reports typically contain a long list of details, especially when reasons are of a safety nature and linked to maintenance issues. The following operational report describes the two days long disruptions originally caused by an aircraft technical problem. It illustrates the complexity of the H24 processes revealing what is happening behind the scenes when aircraft become unserviceable several hours before departure, while passengers are heading to catch their flight.

Early on Day 1 an aircraft that was due to depart at 10:30am underwent an unscheduled maintenance check. The originally reported problem with nose leg bolts was postponed for the following day due to a more urgent hydraulic leak rectification, causing two hours flight delay on two sectors. Next day, soon after midnight, the aircraft was finally taken for repair. A series of events started to unfold resulting in eight hours long passenger delays, while the aircraft was grounded for two days causing costly knock-on effects. Here are the details of the case that could apply to any airline.

| Day 1 | |
|---|---|
| 05:10 | Unscheduled check on aircraft are all going according to plan. After work is done, aircraft will require runs and then the work will be required on nose leg bolts. This may cause slight delay on the next flight. Next OPS (Operations Center) shift will give new estimate after handover. |
| 06:40 | Maintrol (*Line Maintenance and Aircraft Control*) advised, in addition to the nose wheel bolts, which have to be done until midnight, aircraft now has hydraulic leak from undercarriage bay, which they are unable to locate at the moment. No estimate for serviceability can be given, so further information has been requested by departure time (STD 10:30). Crew is placed on Standby report (to protect their flight time limitations). |
| 07:50 | Hydraulic leak found on one of hydraulic system filter bowl. Spare is available. Engineers will advise when leak is rectified and crew will than be called in. While the crews are en route, aircraft needs to be taken out of hangar and post check system idle run will be carried out. |
| 08:30 | Maintrol advised that O ring has been finished. They just need to top up hydraulic fluid, pressurized the tank for idle run and then aircraft will be taken across to stand. Estimating 1–2 hours delay. |
| 08:45 | Maintrol advised, hydraulic leak now fixed, aircraft to be taken out of hangar and idle runs to be completed. Crews have been called in from standby report, ETD 11:45. |

| 10:30 | Scheduled departure time missed |
|---|---|
| 11:00 | Airport Coordination advises aircraft only just being brought onto stand. Handling agent did not have extra tug driver available until now to bring aircraft over from the hangar (all drivers were busy with other aircraft), and the stand was not available, as the aircraft was off the schedule. Engine idle runs still to be carried out. New ETD 12:30. |
| 11:20 | Maintrol advise aircraft on stand and serviceable. |
| 12:30 | Aircraft departed with two hours delays. |
| 22:40 | Aircraft did the flights and arrived back. 2 hours delay outbound/inbound. |

Day 2

| 01:00 | Maintrol advising: during Maintenance Alert check on a nose leg they were not able to tighten bolts. They are required to remove nose landing gear inner cylinder to change bolts. Special tool is needed and will be dispatched from the other base by ground transport. No time was given when this would be completed. Await further info, aircraft planed to operate on Flight 1234, but will change its flight to protect hours. |
|---|---|
| 02:50 | They are still trying to tighten bolts and attempting to avoid removal of inner cylinder due to volume of work, hangar and manpower requirements, will advise further as soon as possible. |
| 04:40 | Maintrol advises it is unlikely aircraft will be serviceable today, due to nose leg investigation/rectification. |
| 06:00 | OPS asked Maintrol if the aircraft can operate scheduled flight today, and then they could have the aircraft for maintenance until lunchtime tomorrow. Maintrol responded that was not possible, as aircraft manufacturer would not give a concession other than a one off positioning flight (with no passengers). Therefore, Flight 1234 ETA now 15:30 (8:00 hours delay), on a first available aircraft. |
| 10:30 | Following Maintrol meeting, last situation is that aircraft is now in a state where it cannot be flown even with gear down. It has to be put in a hangar and on jacks for rectification. Earliest space in hangar is available at 16:00 tomorrow. Based on this, aircraft will be earliest available in 48 hours, if things progress well. The commercial department were advised to look at the flying programme for tomorrow and possibly the day after and to find a replacement aircraft. |

# Appendix 3
# Crew Shortage

A European airline with an extensive network consisting of ten crew bases and seven different aircraft types and versions experienced a series of problems with crew shortages, which affected airline punctuality. Despite having more flight and cabin crew per aircraft than their competitors, the airline crew productivity was much below competitors' average. The company's strategy was predominantly market driven. It tried to satisfy various market segments paying less attention to operational requirements. As a result, operational performance reached the critical state where numerous long delays started to ruin the airline's reputation. In search for answers to crew-generated issues, the airline carried out a detailed analysis based on the operational side of the problem, focusing on one month of mid-season operations. The analysis revealed a chaotic state in crew planning, where staff was hardly able to cope with constant changes in schedule plans. The following are some of the findings based on this analysis:

- Crew productivity was lower than with the main competitors.
- Flight deck crew flying times were well below legal maximums – 53 per cent of maximum utilisation.
- Crew duty times were closer to legal maximums than flying times – 70 per cent of maximum utilisation for flight deck crew and 61 per cent for cabin crew.
- Ground duty times represented more than 60 per cent of duty times for flight deck crew and about 58 per cent for cabin crew.
- Crew qualification at base airports did not match qualification requirements.
- Higher rank crew operated lower ranks 600 times.
- Out-of-base activities on long-haul routes mostly related to days off (55 per cent of total out-of-base activities) and standby duties (35 per cent of total).
- About 67 per cent of these activities were located at two overseas airports.
- Deadhead and positioning activities reached high numbers (1,950 deadhead and 250 positioning flights). This was reflected in high cost of air and ground crew transfer, and hotel accommodation of about €80 per block hour.
- More than 15 per cent of assigned activities were different from actual activities due to changes in flight schedule.
- Flying duty was exceeded by off-duty man-days. The share of days off in total off-duty man-days during the Summer period was as high as 48 per cent, followed by leave (17 per cent), and trip related days off (14 per cent).

- Two out of ten main bases accounted for 69 per cent of total duty hours. However, crew productivity at these airports was the lowest of all in terms of both block and duty hours.

As a consequence, within one month of operations crew shortages caused delays on 42 flights, of which 17 were reactionary delays hidden behind code 93. The average delay amounted to five hours and the longest one departed 20 hours late. On several of the busiest routes, less than 30 per cent of flights operated on-time, with an average delay of one hour.

The Operations Department was trying hard to solve these problems, but without success. Scheduling Department was too busy with numerous other issues and tried to avoid 'unnecessary' work. Preoccupied with their own problems people from the Network Planning Department did not bother much to get involved in 'crewing' problems, while airline strategists were looking to provide capacities for further expansion, and were not keen to get involved in 'details' at operational level. Senior managers did not put much effort to coordinate this process of cross-functional nature.

As a result, the problems continued to accumulate and operational performance further deteriorated. After several serious disruption events which attracted media attention, the company decided to take the problem more seriously, and focused on frontline punctuality improvements. Even then, none of the top managers was directly involved in coordinating the programme. The company's management information system relied on standard operational parameters and financial reports which could not reveal the real causes of problems. In the meantime, the costs started to rise out of control.

# Appendix 4
# Cost Saving and Cultural Issues

In search for simplification of processes and improved operational and cost efficiency, many airlines opt for short-term gains by introducing the *cost saving projects*, which became the euphemism for *cut in labour costs*. They inspire frustration, even cynicism in people all too aware of the real objectives of every new *cost saving project*. The following is one of these cases.

Some years ago, a major airline organised the 'process simplification' project aimed at improvements in airline operational and cost efficiency. The project team was led by the senior manager with support of an external consultant appointed by the CEO. Managers of every single department were involved and participated in numerous tasks set by the central project team. Towards the end of the three months of intensive activities many of the team members and departmental managers started to suspect that behind the whole project was a pre-emptive decision of top management to reduce management numbers. It soon became obvious to the managers and staff across the airline that the three months' long project had not been introduced to bring simplification and improved efficiency of airline processes, but was closely linked with the final stages of a budget plan with a predetermined amount of costs that needed to be cut. The assessment proved correct, for soon after the project ended, the company announced massive redundancies, where hundreds of managers lost their jobs.

The company's culture changed – internal distrust, disputes, and power struggles became a daily occurrence. Driven by an 'unhealthy' working environment and attracted by generous severance packages, some of the key people voluntarily left the company – their contribution in planning, finance, IT and operations was soon greatly missed. The trust in management was lost and this and many other measures that followed were met with cynical distrust affecting the workforce's attitude towards the cost-saving measures. Years of lay-offs that followed, brought the airline into an unenviable situation, with clearly visible consequences on operational performance. Incompetence prevailed together with an autocratic management style. The airline was more frequently experiencing massive disruptions, including long flight delays and numerous cancellations, causing lots of inconvenience to passengers. The relationship gap between top management on one side and employees on the other, widened so much that it attracted a great deal of public attention, putting the airline's overall reputation at risk.

# Appendix 5
# Disruption Audit

An airline was faced with an increasingly high level of disrupted operations. Senior managers were keen to do whatever it takes to decrease the number of operational changes that have obviously contributed to already high losses. The management team decided to carry out a pilot project, thoroughly examine three days of heavy disruptions, find out the volume of costs involved, and more importantly, get to the root causes of the problem beyond codes published in the delay report. The following example illustrates the scope of information that was obtained by using the randomised approach to evaluate management issues hidden behind these disruptions.

## Event Description

At the beginning of the winter schedule, several aircraft were pulled out of service by the maintenance department for unscheduled maintenance without any previous notice. Disruptions were of a large scale and it took the airline six days to return to normal operations. The following information was obtained through the disruption information system, and was partly based on the reconstruction of events in order to reinstate missing data and erroneous inputs.

## Disruption Report

| | |
|---|---|
| Number of disrupted flights | 97 |
| Direct causes of disruptions | 61 per cent Unscheduled maintenance – 6 events caused changes on 35 sectors |
| | 38 per cent Late aircraft delivery – two events caused changes on 24 sectors |
| | 1 per cent Late crew boarding |
| Cancelled flights | 4 (Passenger numbers not available,) |
| Subchartered flights | 22 |
| Crew positioning | 27 (flights/ground) |
| Aircraft positioning | 10 flights |
| Aircraft utilisation | 98 aircraft hours out of service |

| Passengers | 4950 passengers experienced delays over 30min |
| | 2120 passengers experienced delays over 2h |
| | 593 passengers experienced delays over 8h |
| Compensation | 257 passengers from cancelled flights received compensation |
| Total disruption costs, 3 days | €255,600 |
| Cost breakdown | €124,200 Hired  replacement aircraft |
| | €47,600 Additional technical, ferry and sub-positioning flights |
| | €35,600 Cost of passenger delays |
| | €24,100 Diversions (3 flights including positioning) |
| | €14,600 Passenger compensations on cancelled flights |
| | €7,400 Crew cost repositioning |
| | €2,100 Other |

In addition, a thorough root cause analysis was carried out by talking to people who were directly and indirectly involved in this case – COO, Ground Operations, Operations Control, Maintenance Control, Crew Planning, Financial Services and Reservation – which took less than a week. The following are extracts from the report related to direct and indirect causes of disruptions.

*Root cause analysis*

After an in-depth analysis of factual information and reconstruction of events by operational decision makers, the focus was shifted from purely 'technical' reasons, towards the less tangible system issues.

*Management issues*   Senior management are not much involved in resolving operational issues, apart from discussions at weekly delay meetings. There is a lack of interdepartmental coordination, which affects operational results. Without much instruction about the priorities in decision making, the Operations Department is tacitly given the authority to make costly decisions, almost on a daily basis. Responsibilities are not clearly defined. Staff do not have a clear picture about who is doing what and how their decisions influence other processes. There is a lot of improvisation made by inexperienced staff, with much use of a trial and error approach to solve problems, sometimes with harsh operational consequences. A blame culture is preventing many of these matters from being resolved. Many serious issues are not discussed with management. Responsibilities for schedule changes between the Scheduling and Operations departments are not clearly defined and this is reflected in the number and volume of disruptions. Supervision is rare and inconsistent. The management reporting system does not systematically provide enough information related to operational issues. Communication links are weak, especially between Scheduling, Operations, and Maintenance functions.

There is almost no control over outsourced services including financial control.

*Network and schedule planning*   Problems were revealed at several airports and routes, mainly relating to short turn times, late arrivals at airports with night curfews, and inappropriate block times. For example, problems with turnaround times on inbound flights from a major airport resulted in extremely low punctuality of 46 per cent, compared with 76 per cent on outbound sectors, resulting in cascading effects on other flights.

*Operations Control Centre (OCC)*   Lacking clear instructions from senior level, operations managers have set up internal priorities for schedule recovery, which are applied whenever the flight is more than four hours delayed. The first action on their 'recovery list' is flight cancellation, followed by aircraft rental. However, these policies are not always applied due to a fear of incurring high costs. Decisions are made with hesitation and by the time they are resolved, often by cancelling flights, new problems would occur, creating even bigger issues. There is a high number of hidden errors present in almost every area of operations. This results in, for example, numerous crew changes as a consequence of input errors and omissions that occur during the frequent schedule changes. In addition, the accuracy of movement messages is questionable due to erroneous manual inputs. Information about delay reasons is often entered inaccurately and is not descriptive enough, which prevents analysis. There is lack of discipline in filling up voyage reports which affect the quality of operational information. In complex operational situations, OCC expects instructions from a higher level, while the higher level expects recommendations from OCC. These unresolved issues create additional pressure on operations controllers and are the causes of unnecessary disruptions. There is a problem with communication inside the OCC department, where email is the main way of communication even for people seating next to each other. Discussions about issues that need to be resolved collectively are rare. Problems with the exchange of information between Operations and Ground Operations staff are ongoing, where Ground Operations often complain that they do not receive on-time information on disruptions from OCC, citing this as the reason for their late actions.

*Ground operations*   The quality of service at outstations is poorly managed by third parties and is not properly supervised, causing additional inconvenience to already stressed disrupted passengers. The control of invoicing by third parties at outstations is non-existent: hotel accommodation, meals, and transport costs during operational disruptions are fully controlled by agents without any feedback to the airline. The refund policy is defined but there are problems with its implementation. Procedures in the Airline Services Procedures Manual (ASP) are not being updated regularly, resulting in inconsistent services. The ASP Manual is not consistent with the 'Conditions of Carriage' used by the Call Centre. Ground Operations managers are unaware of the volume of irregularities at base airports and outstations and their effects on passengers and costs. Commercial priorities are not specified. Communication with technical bases (third-party service) is sporadic with insufficient control.

*Delay reporting* Delay reports are regularly distributed to the top management team, but contain only essential, unreliable information. Cancelled and diverted flights are not included, nor is the information about the number and costs of hired replacement aircraft. Operational data input is critical, as there are too many errors. Operations people are not fully trained to use the new operations control software.

This was a part of disruption audit that introduced a new approach to disruption management into a troubled airline. It helped the management team to better understand not only the underlying problems of disrupted operations, but also a number of wider, previously unrecognised business issues.

# Appendix 6
# Direct and Indirect Cost of Aircraft Damage

The following examples describe causes and consequences of aircraft damage incidents experienced by two different airlines. The calculation of direct and indirect costs was based on methods for disruption loss management.

**Case 1**

The fuselage of a B747 was damaged by the catering truck at an outstation on a long-haul route. The aircraft was temporarily repaired by a third party and sent back to home base where it was finally repaired after four days. In the meantime, 335 passengers and ten crew members stayed overnight in a hotel and after more than 24 hours' delay were transferred to their destination – 125 passengers travelled by three other carriers, while the remaining passengers were carried by spare aircraft sent from the home base. Other disruptions lasting over the four days included eight reactionary flights using partly spare and partly hired aircraft. The cost of direct damage amounted to €115,000, while the indirect cost including revenue loss to other carriers reached €1.2 million. The calculation was based on the system information about costs, as well as data gathered from the original sources, like the cost of hired aircraft, additional repair required by lessor, and loss of aircraft market value as the aircraft was intended for sale.

**Case 2**

A gouge was found on a B737–500 during a routine check at the base airport. The aircraft was pulled out of service for five days, affecting 39 flights. There were 24 flights operated by a hired aircraft, 11 flights were delayed, the aircraft type was changed on eight sectors and two flights were cancelled. The total duration of the delays was 21 hours and the total number of disrupted passengers was 1,420. The indirect costs of disruptions amounted to €295,000, while the airline spent €19,000 on aircraft repair.

# Bibliography

A report and consultation by the CAA of the Aerodrome Congestion Working Group, Response by British Airways, April 2005.

AEA (2005), 'Punctuality and delay', *Market Research Quarterly* (No. 3).

Air Transport Action Group (2003), 'Fast Facts', <www.atag.org>.

*Airline Business News* (2008), Comment: Immunity jab, 19 August.

*Airports International* (2007), 'Top 100 Airports', March.

Airports Council International (2000), *Air Passenger Rights and the European Union*. European Commission Consultation Document on Air Passenger Rights.

Aspesi, C. and Vardhan, D. (2005), 'Brilliant strategy, but can you execute?', *McKinsey Quarterly*, <www.mckinseyquarterly.com>.

Ayres, I. (2007), *Super Crunchers* (London: John Murray).

Baiada, R.M. (2005), *The Network Airline Production Problem* (ATH Group Inc), p. 25.

Bennis, W., Goleman, D. and O'Toole, J. (2008), *Transparency* (Jossey-Bass).

Bonabeau, E. (2002), 'Predicting the unpredictable', *Harvard Business Review*.

Bourne, M. and Bourne, P. (2004), *Balanced Scorecard in a Week* (London: Hodder & Stoughton).

— (2007), *Change Management* (London: Hodder Arnold).

— (2007), *Balanced Scorecard* (London: Hodder Arnold).

Buehler, K.S. (2003), 'Running with risk', *McKinsey Quarterly*, <www.mckinseyquarterly.com>.

Brown, P. (2003), 'Companies get creative in their inventory management solutions', *Aviation Week*, 15 April.

Bryan, L. (2002), 'Just-in-time strategy for a turbulent world', *McKinsey Quarterly*, <http://www.mckinseyquarterly.com>.

Cammilus, J. (2008), 'Strategy as a wicked problem', *Harvard Business Review*, May.

Capra, F. (1983), *The Turning Point* (Flamingo).

Committee on Commerce, Science, and Transportation of United States Senate in September 2000.

Connell, P. (2005), *Measuring Operational Risk Management Systems under Basel II* (Institute of Internal Auditors), <www.theiia.org/FSAarchive>.

Cooke, D. (2003), *Learning from Incidents* (University of Calgary: Haskayne School of Business).

Costa, P., Harned, D. and Lundquist, J. (2002), 'Rethinking the aviation industry', *McKinsey Quarterly*, <www.mckinseyquarterly.com>.

Courtney, H. (2005), 'Making the most of uncertainty', *McKinsey Quarterly*, <www.mckinseyquarterly.com>.

Darnton, G. with Darnton, M. (1997), *Business Process Analysis* (London: International Thomson Business Press).

Debels, P. *Genspace Project* (Eurocontrol).

Dettmer, H.W. (2000), *Constraint Management – The Complete Guide to the CQM* (Quality America, Inc).

Dobbs, R. and Koller, T. (2005), 'Measuring long-term performance', *McKinsey Quarterly*, <www.mckinseyquarterly.com>.

Doganis, R. (2001), *The Airline Business in the Twenty-first Century* (Routledge).

— (2002), *Flying Off Course* (Routledge).

Doig, S., Howard, A. and Ritter, R. (2003), 'The hidden value in airline operations', *McKinsey Quarterly*, <www.mckinseyquarterly.com>.

DoT US, *Air Travel Consumer Report*, <http://airconsumer.ost.dot.gov/>.

ERA *Departure Punctuality 2001–2006, Overall Performance*, ERA Airline Statistics <www.eraa.org>.

Eurocontrol (2005), *Performance Review Report*, April.

Eurocontrol (2006), *Digest – Annual 2006, Delays to Air Transport in Europe*, <www.eurocontrol.int/eCoda/>.

Eurocontrol (2007), *A Matter of Time: Air Traffic Delay in Europe*, September, <www.eurocontrol.int>.

Eurocontrol PRR (2006), Performance Review Commission Report.

European Commission (2000), *Consultation Paper on a Community Air Passenger Report on Service Quality Indicators*.

Federal Managers Association (2000), Testimony Before the Committee on Commerce, Science, and Transportation, United States Senate, 14 September.

Federal Register Environmental Documents (2002), 'Reporting the Causes of Airline Delays and Cancellations', (US Department of Transportation), <www.epa.gov>.

Field, D. (2007), 'FAA stop over-scheduling', *Airline Business*, September.

Flint, P. (2001), 'Friends again', *Air Transport World*, August.

— *Staying on Time*, September (ATW Online) <www.atwonline.com>.

Foot, M. (2003), *Operational Risk Management – Best Practice Strategies in Light of Final Basel Proposals*, <www.fsa.gov.uk>.

Fostrer, R. and Kaplan, S. (2001), *Creative Destruction* (Doubleday/Currency).

Frappaolo, C. (2002), *Knowledge Management* (Oxford: Capstone Publishing).

Gladwell, M. (2002), *The Tipping Point* (Abacus: New Ed edition).

Gladwell, M. (2005), *Blink* (London: Penguin Group).

Hansson, T., Ringbeck, J. and Franke, M. (2002), *Airlines: A New Operating Model, Providing Service and Coverage Without the Cost Penalty, Strategy + Business* (Booz Allen and Hamilton) <www.boozallen.com>.

Hansson, T., Ringbeck, J. and Franke M (2002), 'Flight for survival: A new operating model for airlines', *Strategy + Business* (Booz Allen and Hamilton) <www.boozallen.com>.

Harmon, E., Hensel, S. and Lukes, T. (2006), 'Measuring performance in services', *McKinsey Quarterly*, <www.mckinseyquarterly.com>.

*Harvard Business Review on Change* (1998), A Harvard Business Review Paperback.

Hauschild, S., Licht, T. and Stein, W. (2001), 'Creating a knowledge culture', *McKinsey Quarterly.*

Heller, R. (1998), *Managing Change* (London: Dorling Kindersley Ltd).

Hitt, M., Hoskisson, R. and Ireland, R.D. (2007), *Management of Strategy* (Thomson South-Western).

Hoffer, Gittell J. (2005), *Southwest Airlines Way* (McGraw-Hill).

IATA (2008), 'IATA Partners With Flight Safety Foundation To Tackle Pilot Shortage', 27 February, IATA.<www.iata.org/pressroom/briefings/2008-02-27-02>.

ITA (2000), *Costs of Air Transport Delay in Europe*, Final Report.

Jameson, R. (2002), 'The true cost of operational risk', *ERisk.com.*

Janic, M. (2005), 'Modeling the large scale disruptions of an airline network', *Journal of Transportation Engineering.*

Jensen, B. (2000), *Simplicity* (London: HarperCollinsBusiness).

Johnston, R. and Clark, G. (2005), *Service Operations Management* (Pearson Education Limited).

Klein, G. (2003), *The Power of Intuition: How to Use Your Gut Feelings to Make Better Decisions at Work* (Doubleday/Currency).

Knorren Nichols, W. and Kunz, M. (1999), 'Hubbing on time', *Airline Business*, August.

Koch, R. (2006), *The 80/20 Principle* (London: Nicholas Brealey Publishing).

Laseter, T. and Kandybin, A. and Houston, P. (2007), 'Marketing and operations: Can this marriage be saved?', *Strategy + Business*, <www.strategy-business.com>.

Laseter, T. and Laseter, L. (2007), 'See for yourself', *Strategy + Business*, <www.strategy-business.com>.

Leslie, K. (2006), 'Managing your organisation by the evidence', *McKinsey Quarterly*, <www.mckinseyquarterly.com>.

Malhotra, Y. (2004), *Why Knowledge Management Systems Fail?* (Syracuse: Syracuse University, School of Management) <www.brint.org/WhyKMSFail.htm>.

Manning, C. and Gross, S., 'The big squeeze', *Strategy + Business*, <www.boozallen.com>.

Mintzberg, H. (2000), *The Rise and Fall of Strategic Planning* (London: FT Prentice Hall).

— (2006), *How Productivity Killed American Enterprise* <www.henrymintzberg.com>.

Mintzberg, H., Ahlstrand, B. and Lampel, J. (2005), *Strategy Bites Back* (Pearson Education Limited).

National Transport Safety Board (1993), NTSB Order No. EA-3853 on Block to block time case.

Niehues, A., Belin, A., Hasson, T., Hauser, R., Mostajo, M. and Richter J (2001), *Punctuality: How Airlines Can Improve On-Time Performance* (Booz Allen and Hamilton).

Palmeri, C. and Epstein, K. (2007), 'Fear & loathing at the airport', *BusinessWeek*, September.

Petraccione, L. (2007), *Delta's Operation Clockwork* (Transportation & Logistics Practice) <www.atwonline.com>.

Rapajic, J. (1993), 'Managing the cost controls', *Airline Business*.

— (2004), 'Hidden costs of your operations', *Regional International, Journal of the European Regions Association*.

Reiley, J. (2006), *Strategy & Performance* (The Telegraph Business Club).

Roxburgh, C. (2003), 'Hidden flows in strategy', *McKinsey Quarterly*, <www.mckinseyquarterly.com>.

Sengel, M. P. (2006), *The Fifth Discipline, The Art and Practice of the Learning Organization* (Double Day).

Slack, N., Chambers, S. and Johnston, R. (2004), *Operations Management* (London: FT Prentice Hall).

Stacey, R. (2007), *Strategic Management and Organisational Dynamics*, 5th edition (London: FT Prentice Hall).

Sutcliffe, K. and Weber, K. (2003), 'The high cost of accurate knowledge', *Harvard Business Review*, May.

Taneja, N. (2002), IATA Information Management Meeting, Orlando.

*The Economist* (2006), The New Organisation, A Survey of the Company, 21st January

The Joint Economic Committee (2008), *Your Flight has been Delayed Again*, Report of the Joint Economic Committee of the US Congress (May), <www.jec.senate.gov>.

Top, W.N. (1991), *Safety and Loss Control Management and the International Safety Rating System* <www.topves.nl>.

Transport Studies Group,(2004), *Evaluating the True Cost to Airlines of One Minute of Airborne or Ground Delay* (London: University of Westminster).

US Department of Transportation (2001), 'Reporting the causes of airline delays and cancellations', *Federal Register*, 27 December (Volume 66, Number 248).

US DoT (2004), Order 7210.55C, Operational Data Reporting Requirements.

Yu, G. and Qi, X (2004), *Disruption Management* (Singapore: World Scientific Publishing Co. Pte Ltd).

# Index

Bold page numbers indicate figures, *italic* numbers indicate tables.

15 minutes grace period 25–6

ACARS (Aircraft Communications Addressing and Reporting System) 27
accessibility of data 78
accountability for disruptions 117
accuracy of data 79–80, 81, 91–2, **92**
add-ons 82
aeronautical information 66
air traffic control (ATC)
  capacity of 64–5
  data capture of flight delays 24
  flight delay reports 30
Air Transport Association (ATA) 27
Air Transport Users Council (AUC) 137–8
aircraft
  automated equipment 26–7
  and causes of disruption 52
  changes 32–3
  damage to 40, 63, 85–6, 134–5, 157
  disruption analysis by 85
  hiring of 33, 41
  purchasing and implementation of 59
Aircraft Communications Addressing and Reporting System (ACARS) 27
airline industry
  external constraints 6–7
  internal constraints 7–10
  management of disruptions across 136–7
  outsourcing of core businesses 7
  public exposure of delay records 31
  safety implications of time pressures 17–18
  uncertainty in operations 69
airlines
  communication between departments 61–2

costs of delays borne by 19
data capture of flight delays 24
organisational culture of 62–3, 118–19, 151
simplification of business models 98–103, **99, 101**
airports
  capacity of 64–5
  data capture of flight delays 24
airspace congestion 65
American Airlines 108–9
analysis of disruptions 84–5
arrival times, data capture of 24
Association of European Airlines (AEA) 28
ATC. *see* air traffic control (ATC)
automated aircraft equipment 26–7
Ayres, Ian 128

benefits from disruptions 19
boundary spanners 116
British Airways **67**, 98, **99**, 101, **101**, 102
budgeting 122
buffers, schedule 24–5, 51
Bureau of Transportation Statistics (BTS) (US) 29

cancellation of flights 31–2
CAPRS Project 11
capturing of data 78–9
causes of disruptions
  data capture for 43–4
  and errors in delay reporting 44–6, *45*
  IATA delay coding system 42–3, *43, 144–6*
  as multiple and intangible 42
  *see also* hidden causes of disruption
Civil Aviation Authority (CAA) UK 28
coding of routes 83
coding system for delays (IATA) 42–3, *43, 144–6*
collection of data 78–9
communication

cross-functional 61–2
in disruption management 117–18
between operational/strategic levels
8–9
compensation for passengers, regulation
concerning 137–8
completeness of data 81–2
complexity of organisations 69–70,
98–103, **99, 101**
Confidential Human Factors Incident
Reporting Programme (CHIRP)
17–18
congestion 65, 66
Continental Airlines **48**, 109, 128
control of operations 126
coordination at industry-level 68
cost cutting 60, 133–4, *134*
cost of disruptions 74
aircraft damage 40
allocation to disruption events 41, *42*
borne by airlines and passengers 19
crew costs 40
current cost management 34, *35,* 36–7
data on 79–80
defining 37–8
delta costs 38–41, *39*
estimates of 34
handling charges 40
hired aircraft 41
lack of information on 13, 15, *16*
landing charges 40
passenger costs 40
punctuality costs 38, *39*
revenue loss 41
route costs 39–40
cost savings and cultural issues 151
crews
cost of accommodation 79
costs 40
planning 54, 56, 127
safety implications of disruptions 64
shortages 149–50
cross-functional communication 61–2
culture, organisational 62–3, 118–19, 151

damage to aircraft 40, 63, 85–6, 134–5,
157
data

accessibility 78
accuracy 79–80, 81
accuracy of 91–2, **92**
capture 23–4, 26–7, 42–5, *45,* 78–9
completeness of 81–2
identification of 77–8
input 80–1, 87
integration with sources of 87–8
links 81
maintenance and update of 77–8, 87
organisation of 77–83
quality of 78
technology and integration of 87–91
updating 80–1
decision-making
as cause of disruption 53, 147–8
fast 57–8
on investment 55
and system knowledge of staff 59
using disruption loss management
system 114–15, **115**
delay coding system (IATA) 42–3, *43,*
144–6
delay meetings 8
delay reports
data capture for 26–7
inadequacy of 10–11, *12,* 13, *14, 15*
lack of cost implications 13, 15, *16*
delays
errors in reporting 44–5, *45*
flight 22–3
information on 22–3
passenger perspective 30–1
public exposure of records 31
sources of public information on
28–30
Delta Air Lines 100–1
delta costs 38–41, *39*
departure times, data capture of 24
disruption loss management system
accessibility of data 78
accuracy of data 79–80, 91–2, **92**
add-ons 82
analysis of disruptions 84–5
benefits of 95
coding of routes 83
collection of data 78–9
completeness of data 81–2

cost alerts 83
data links 81
decision-making using 114–15, **115**
event escapability 82–3
and expansion of the airline industry
    6–7
and external constraints 6–7
filtering of information 82
identification of data 77–8
as important business strategy 5
information requirements 74–5
information structure **75,** 75–7
input of data 80–1, 87
integration with data sources 87–8
integration with other systems 88–9
and internal constraints 7–10
loss recovery module 85–6
main system functions **83,** 83–7
maintenance of data 77–8, 87
monitoring of disruptions 84
organisation of data 77–83
overview of system scheme 89–91,
    **90**
platform 88
quality of data 78
quick start 79
relational maps 93–5, **94**
reports from the system 84
scenario builder 86–7
updating data 80–1
validation and system audit 81
as web application 88
disruption management
accountability 117
and communication 117–18
and culture of the organisation 118–19
information management 115–16
learning through 119
disruption risk management 129–31, **131**
disruptions
causes of 41–6, *43, 45*
cost of 34–41
effects on service providers 66
escapability 82–3
growing problems with 47
management of across the industry
    136–7
management through 131–3, 153–6
operational events 22–33
    *see also* hidden causes of disruption
diverted flights 32

easyjet 98, **99**
efficiency and network systems 49–50
employees
failure to provide information to 63
and hidden agendas of management 63
safety implications of disruptions 64
system knowledge of 59–60
environment, implications of disruptions
    for 18
errors in reporting of delays 44–5, *45*
escapability 82–3
Eurocontrol 28–9
European Aviation Safety Agency (EASA)
    29–30
European Commission CAPRS Project 11
European Regions Airline Association
    (ERAA) 28
European Union and passenger protection
    17, 137
event escapability 82–3
executive reports 84
expansion
of the airline industry 6–7
as driver of disruptions 47, 50
external constraints 6–7

fast decision-making 57–8
15 minutes grace period 25–6
filtering of information 82
financial reporting, inadequacy of 13, 15,
    *16*
fleet
planning 124
utilisation 52
flexibility of reports 82
flight cancellations 31–2
flight delays
ambiguities in reports of 23–4
and data capture 23–4, 26–7
information on 22–3
passenger perspective 24
public exposure of records 31
schedule buffers 24–5
sources of public information on 28–30

unreported 25–6
flights
    additional 33
    cancellations of 31–2
    diverted 32
focus of management 103–5
fuel consumption
    calculation of costs 79
    cost saving measures 37

gathering of data 78–9
goodwill loss due to disruptions 41
grace period 25–6
ground services 65, 127–8
growth as driver of disruptions 47, 50

handling charges 40
Heathrow, decline in punctuality 66, **67**
hidden causes of disruption
    aeronautical information 66
    aircraft-related issues 52
    airline culture 62–3, 118–19, 151
    cost cutting measures 60
    crew planning 54
    cross-functional communication 61–2
    effects of disruptions on service
        providers 66
    external issues 64–8
    fast decision-making 57–8
    ground services 65
    imbalance in management power 58
    investment decisions 55
    lack of industry-level coordination 68
    lack of system knowledge by staff
        59–60
    marketing 54
    operational decisions 53, 147–8
    outsourcing 55–6
    punctuality targets 60
    regulatory issues 67
    safety implications 64
    sales 54
    scheduling 50–1
    software and IT 56–7
    strategy 48–9
    system functions 48–57
    taxi-out delays 66–7
    third party damages 63

time usage by senior managers 57
    traffic congestion 64–5
hired aircraft, costs of 41
hiring of aircraft 33
Hoffer Gittel, J. 108
hub-and-spoke networks 49–50, 64, 123
hybrid airlines 102

IATA delay coding system 42–3, *43*, 144–6
identification of data 77–8
imbalance in management power 58
indirect causes of disruption. *see* hidden
    causes of disruption
industry-level coordination 68
information
    about delay causes 42–5, *45*
    aeronautical 66
    for cost management 36–7
    on delays 22–3
    failure to provide to staff 63
    filtering of 82
    on flight cancellations 32
    on flight diversions 32
    management of 115–16
    public sources of 28–30
information systems
    benefits of 72–4
    current inadequacy of 9–10
    current solutions 70–2
    delay information 22–3
    events not recorded 27
    inadequacy of financial reporting 13,
        15, *16*
    and network planning 124
    route planning and pricing 125
    and schedule planning 124–5
    *see also* disruption loss management
        system
input of data 80–1
integration
    with data sources 87–8
    of data with technology 87–91
    with other systems 88–9
internal constraints 7–10
International Air Transport Organisation
    (ICAO) 29
Internet information providers 29
investment decisions 55

IT as cause of disruption 56–7

key disruption indicators (KDI) 114
knowledge
    of disruption causes 9–11, *12,* 13, *14,*
        *15*
    of the system 59–60
Koch, Richard 98, 102

labour costs, implications of cutting 59, 60
landing charges 40
learning through disruption management
    119, 131–3
legacy airlines 100–1
links, data 81
loss management
    and cost cutting 133–4, *134*
    management through disruptions
        131–3
    operations 126–9
    planning 122–6
    quality control 135–6
    recovery of losses 134–5, 157
    revenue loss control 128–9
    risk management 129–31, **131**
low-cost carriers 49–50, 99–100, 102
Lufthansa 55–6

maintenance
    as cause of disruption 52
    of data 77–8
    and loss management 127
management
    communication between levels 8–9
    current approach to cost management
        34, *35,* 36–7
    of disruptions 114–15, **115**
    of disruptions across the industry
        136–7
    focus of 103–5
    hidden agendas of 63
    power imbalances 58
    questions for DLM system 114–15,
        **115**
    through disruptions 131–3, 153–6
    time usage by senior managers 57
    *see also* disruption loss management
        system; disruption management;

    loss management; performance
        measurement
maps, relational 93–5, **94**
marketing as cause of disruption 54
measurement, performance
    and accountability for disruptions 117
    defining measures 110–11, *112–14,* 114
    of disruption causes 107–10
    key disruption indicators (KDI) 114
    need for focus in 106–7
    objectives of 106
    suppliers 126
Mintzberg, Henri 60
monitoring of disruptions 84

network planning 123–4
network systems, efficiency of 49–50
Niehues, A. 49

operational constraints
    external 6–7
    internal 7–10
    and planning 6
operational decisions as cause of disruption
    53, 147–8
operational events as disruptions
    additional flights 33
    aircraft changes 32–3
    aircraft hire 33
    analysis of 85
    in disruption information system 75–7,
        *76*
    diverted flights 32
    flight cancellations 31–2
    flight delays 22–31
operational management
    communication with strategic level
        8–9
    and loss management 126–9
optimisation tools for crew planning 56
organisation of data 77–83
organisational culture 62–3, 151
organising 115
outsourcing 7, 55–6, 126

padded schedules 51
passengers
    costs of delays borne by 19

and delays 30–1
    disruption costs related to 40
    and flight delays 24
    goodwill loss due to disruptions 41
    implications for of disruptions 15, 17
    regulation concerning compensation
        137–8
performance measurement
    and accountability for disruptions 117
    defining measures 110–11, *112–14*, 114
    of disruption causes 107–10
    key disruption indicators (KDI) 114
    need for focus in 106–7
    objectives of 106
    suppliers 126
pilots
    safety implications of disruptions 64
    shortage of 54
planning
    crew 54, 127
    in loss management 122–6
    and operational constraints 6
    self-induced risks through 7–8
profitability and punctuality of flights 49
punctuality of flights
    ambiguities in reports of 23–4
    costs 38, *39*
    deterioration in 47, **47**, 66–7, **67**
    information on 22–3
    and low-cost carriers 49
    and profitability 49
    schedule buffers 22–325–6
    and simple business models 98–102,
        **99, 101**
    targets 60
    unreported delays 23–4
purchasing of aircraft 59

quality control 135–6
quality of data 77–8, 78

regulation
    as cause of disruption 67
    concerning passenger compensation
        137–8
relational maps 93–5, **94**
reporting of delays, errors in 44–5, *45*
reports from the system 82, 84

reports on delays
    ambiguities in 23–4
    data capture for 26–7
    inadequacy of 10–11, *12*, 13, *14, 15*
    lack of cost implications 13, 15, *16*
revenue loss
    control of 128–9
    due to disruptions 41
risk management 129–31, **131**
risks
    safety 17–18
    self-induced through planning 7–8
routes
    coding 83
    costs 39–40
    planning and pricing of 125–6
Ryanair 49, 51, 98, **99**

safety implications of disruptions 17–18, 64
sales as cause of disruption 54
scenario builder 86–7, 126
schedule buffers 24–5, 51
schedules
    as cause of disruption 50–1
    planning 124–5
self-induced risks 7–8
service suppliers 55–6, 66, 126
Silverjet 101, **101**
simplification of business processes
        98–103, **99, 101**
software and IT as causes of disruption
        56–7
sources of information, public 28–30
Southwest Airlines **48**, 102, 108, 109
*Southwest Airlines Way, The* (Hoffer Gittel)
        108
spare part policies 52
staff
    failure to provide information to 63
    and hidden agendas of management 63
    safety implications of disruptions 64
    system knowledge of 59–60
Stamp, Sir Josiah 10–11
strategic management
    communication with operational level
        8–9
    as disruption cause 48–50
    dynamic 122–3

planning  7
*Super Crunchers* (Ayres)  128
suppliers, service  55–6, 126
system audit  81
system functions as disruption causes
    aircraft-related issues  52
    crew planning  54
    investment decisions  55
    marketing  54
    operational decisions  53, 147–8
    outsourcing  55–6
    sales  54
    scheduling  50–1
    strategy  48–50
system knowledge of staff  59–60

tarmac delays  27, 66–7
taxi-out delays  66–7
technical disruptions and loss management
    127
technology
    as cause of disruption  56–7
    and data integration  87–91
    DLM platform  88
    improvements in delay reporting  26–7
third party damages  63, 134–5

time pressures and safety  17–18
time usage by senior managers  57
traffic congestion  64–5

uncertainty in airline operations  69
United Airlines  **48**, 109
United States
    Bureau of Transportation Statistics
        (BTS)  29
    delay cause reporting  80–1
    delay reporting in  11, *12,* 13
    traffic congestion  64–5
    use of Aircraft Communications
        Addressing and Reporting System
        (ACARS)  27
unreported flight delays  25–6
update of data  77–8
updating data  80–1

validation audit  81

web application, system as  88

*Your Flight Has Been Delayed Again*
    (Joint Economic Committee of US
    Congress)  34

# Other titles from Ashgate

**Flying Ahead of the Airplane**
Nawal K. Taneja
2008 • 298 pages
Hardback
978-0-7546-7579-2

**Straight and Level:**
**Practical Airline Economics, 3rd edition**
Stephen Holloway
2008 • 614 pages
Hardback/Paperback
978-0-7546-7256-2/978-0-7546-7258-6

**Aviation Project Management**
Triant G. Flouris and Dennis Lock
2008 • 314 pages
Hardback
978-0-7546-7395-8

**Airline Marketing and Management, 6th edition**
Stephen Shaw
2007 • 336 pages
Hardback/Paperback
978-0-7546-3758-5/ 978-0-7546-3759-2

**Airline Finance, 3rd Edition**
Peter S. Morrell
2007 • 260 pages
Hardback/Paperback
978-0-7546-7000-1/ 978-0-7546-7134-3

# ASHGATE